Marketing Logistics

Marketing Logistics

Second edition

Martin Christopher and Helen Peck

AMSTERDAM BOSTON HEIDELBERG LONDON NEW YORK OXFORD
PARIS SAN DIEGO SAN FRANCISCO SINGAPORE SYDNEY TOKYO

Butterworth-Heinemann
An imprint of Elsevier
Linacre House, Jordan Hill, Oxford OX2 8DP
200 Wheeler Road, Burlington, MA 01803

First published 1997
Second edition 2003

British Library Cataloguing in Publication Data
Christopher, Martin
    Marketing logistics. – 2nd ed.
    1. Marketing – Management
    I. Title   II. Peck, Helen
    658.5

Library of Congress Cataloguing in Publication Data
A catalogue record for this book is available from the Library of Congress

ISBN 0 7506 5224 1

For information on all Butterworth-Heinemann publications visit our
website at: www.bh.com

Composition by Genesis Typesetting Limited, Rochester, Kent
Printed and bound in Great Britain by Biddles Ltd. www.biddles.co.uk

Contents

Preface

When the first edition of this book was published, it was already clear that the traditional concept of marketing was being challenged. This challenge arose from the realisation that the environment in which the original frameworks and principles of marketing had been formulated had changed significantly. Instead of a situation where demand exceeded supply – a condition which persisted in some markets until quite late into the twentieth century – it was clear that the reverse condition was more often the norm.

This transition from a sellers' market to a buyers' market meant that the conventional focus in many companies on the classic '4 Ps' of Product, Price, Promotion and Place had to be radically reviewed. Now there is widespread recognition that companies compete not so much through what they do, but through how they do it. In other words, the ways in which key business processes are managed and how those processes are aligned with the needs of the market can be every bit as important as the quality of the product or its price.

Emerging from this changed competitive landscape has come the idea that the processes that enable demand to be fulfilled in a more responsive and reliable way can be critical to the achievement of market-place success. Of equal importance is the way in which relationships are managed, both upstream and downstream of the company. These three 'Rs' – Responsiveness, Reliability and Relationships – underpin the idea of marketing logistics.

Marketing logistics focuses upon the ways in which customer service can be leveraged to gain competitive advantage. It seeks to manage the interface between the marketing and logistics activities of the organisation in order to align their respective strategies within the context of the wider supply chain.

Traditionally, marketing and logistics have been managed separately within most businesses. The linkages between the two have been poorly understood, and the strategic importance of customer service was, until recently, not always recognised. As markets become 'commoditised' and as customers become more time and service sensitive, the need to manage the marketing and logistics interface increases.

The convergence of marketing and logistics is based upon a simple model that recognises the three key arenas that need to be strategically connected: the consumer franchise, customer value, and the supply chain.

In writing this second edition of *Marketing Logistics* we have sought to develop the idea that, within the business, the two areas of demand creation (marketing) on the one hand and demand fulfilment (logistics) on the other should not be seen as separate functions but should be brought together through the mechanisms of supply chain management.

The aim is to create a market-driven supply chain strategy whereby customer and consumer value is delivered in the most efficient and effective way.

In producing this short book, we have been influenced by the ideas and research of our colleagues in the Cranfield School of Management, where marketing and logistics have long been seen to be closely interconnected. Particular thanks should be given to Tracy Stickells, who has worked hard to craft the manuscript through many drafts.

Martin Christopher
Helen Peck

Chapter 1

The new market place

In many Western economies the dynamics of the market place have changed in recent years. Markets are increasingly characterised by sophisticated and demanding customers and consumers, within a competitive environment that is far more volatile and less predictable than before. Under these conditions marketing's reliance on the classic '4 Ps' of product, price, promotion and place is no longer sufficient to achieve market leadership. Instead, winning companies are those that can speed up the rate of innovation, bring new products and services to the market place faster, and replenish demand in shorter lead times and with greater reliability – in short, these companies are more *responsive*. Creating the responsive organisation has to be the main priority of management in any business, and achieving it requires a much greater focus on the *processes* through which demand is met. This is the arena of marketing logistics – the critical interface between the market place and the organisation seeking to satisfy customer requirements.

In recent years there has been a growing questioning of the effectiveness of marketing as it has conventionally been practised. Whilst the basic principles of marketing still hold – that is, the identification of customer needs and the satisfaction of them at a profit to the supplier – there is some doubt as to whether the focus of 'traditional' marketing upon branding and positioning is still appropriate. In this classic model the routes to competitive advantage have typically been based upon strong brands, corporate images, media advertising and, in some cases, price. These are the classic components of conventional marketing strategies. In today's turbulent market place, however, it is no longer sufficient to have attractive products, competitively priced and creatively advertised. There has been a growing tendency for customers to want more – specifically, to require ever-higher levels of service.

Customer service has become the competitive battleground in many industries. It can provide a significant opportunity to differentiate an otherwise standard product and to tailor the company's offering to meet specific customer requirements.

This trend towards the *service-sensitive* customer is as apparent in industrial markets as it is in consumer markets. Hence companies supplying the car industry, for example, must be capable of providing just-in-time deliveries direct to the assembly line; similarly, a food manufacturer supplying a large supermarket chain must have an equivalent logistics capability, enabling it to keep the retail shelf filled whilst minimising the amount of inventory in the system. The evidence from across a range of markets suggests that a critical determinant of whether orders are won or lost, and hence the basis for becoming a preferred supplier, is customer service. Time has become a far more critical element in the competitive process. Customers in every market want ever-shorter lead times; product availability often overcomes brand or supplier loyalty – meaning that if the customer's preferred brand is not available and a substitute is, then the likelihood is a lost sale.

The changing marketing environment

It has to be recognised that there have been some radical changes in the marketing environment since marketing first came to prominence in the early 1960s. Fifty years ago, organisations that had even the most rudimentary understanding of the marketing concept were able to reap the harvest of fast-growing markets comprising customers who had money to spend. In such conditions it was easy to believe that the company's marketing effort was the main driver of this success. In reality, that success was due as much to the fact that the business was being carried along with the tidal wave of market growth.

The most significant change to impact on Western companies since that time has been the maturing of the markets in which they compete. Mature markets have certain characteristics that mark them out as being significantly different from growth markets, and chief amongst these are:

- Sophisticated and experienced customers
- Perceived equality of product functionality
- Transition from a sellers' market to a buyers' market
- Price competition.

Customer sophistication

In the majority of Western economies, today's customers and consumers have seen it all – they have been there and 'bought the T-shirt'. In industrial markets, as well as fast-moving consumer goods markets, the supplier is now faced with a buyer who is much more demanding and less easily persuaded by marketing 'hype'. One consequence of this change is the gradual decline in brand loyalty in many markets. Brand *loyalty* has been replaced by brand *preference*. What this means is that the buyer may prefer to buy a particular product from a particular supplier for a variety of reasons – for example, physical characteristics, attributes, convenience, etc. However, this is not the same as loyalty. If, for example, a product is out of stock on the shelf, are shoppers willing to take another brand? Often they are. Or if an original equipment manufacturer finds that delivery lead times from one supplier are not as reliable as those provided by a competitor, then the likelihood is that the business will switch. Buyers in industrial markets are increasingly subjecting suppliers to rigorous 'vendor appraisals', and will switch suppliers if performance fails to meet their requirements – knowing that a product of equivalent technical quality is available from alternative sources.

Perceived product equality

Mature markets exhibit similar characteristics to commodity markets in that customers perceive little difference between competing offers. In such conditions, as we have suggested, if the preferred brand is not available, customers will willingly accept a substitute. Even products/ markets with high rates of innovation do not seem immune from this tendency to 'commoditisation'; take, for example, the personal computer market, where clones and 'me-too's' now account for significant market shares.

Transition from a sellers' to a buyers' market

Previously manufacturers tended to be the dominant force, as they 'pushed' products into a fragmented market place. Over the last few decades there has been a major swing in the balance of power in the distribution channel. Globalisation has further eroded manufacturer power as barriers to market entry from new sources of competition have been removed through the liberalisation of trade. As a result, customers today are less passive and are faced with greater choice.

Power in the distribution channel tends to reside with whoever has the strongest relationship with the end-user. In the past it was the manufacturer who had that relationship through its brand. Today the end-user is more likely to have a closer relationship with the retailer, whose own brand loyalty is in the ascendancy as traditional manufacturer brand loyalty declines. Conventionally, in consumer marketing particularly, advertising has long been seen as a means of building differential advantage. Whilst there can be no question that a strong media presence provides a foundation for market-place success, it seems that more and more decisions are taken at the point of purchase, suggesting that on-the-shelf presence is as important as media presence. Put another way, 'share-of-shelf' is as critical as 'share-of-voice'.

Price competition

Almost by definition, the combined effect of the previous three factors is a downward pressure on price. As a result, there is a temptation to pursue tactical gains in sales volume through discounting in one form or another, which is compounded by the continuing demands for price reductions by powerful customers. Paradoxically, the more that organisations compete on price, the more they reinforce the customers' view that they are indeed commodity suppliers.

Price deflation is likely to be as big a concern in the current decade as inflation was in previous years. Overcapacity exists on a worldwide scale in most industries, and where supply exceeds demand there is an inevitable downward pressure on price. The implications of falling real prices are significant. If margins are to be maintained, then obviously costs must fall at least as fast as prices. Thus it may be expected that retailers, for example, will be placing even more pressure on their suppliers for further price reductions. Equally, original equipment manufacturers such as car assembly companies will be looking to component suppliers to reduce their prices.

The commoditisation of the computer industry

In the early 1960s, IBM controlled 70 per cent of the computer market through its disparate range of incompatible computers. Customers – large corporations, governmental or institutional bodies – leased rather than bought the colossally expensive machines. Periodically, they would upgrade or replace them. The change inevitably subjected the customer to the expense of rewriting programs, regardless of whether the replacement machine was provided by IBM or a competitor. Wishing to reduce the risk of customer defections at this critical juncture, IBM standardised its programming in 1964, giving customers a real incentive to stay with 'Big Blue'. In doing so, IBM created an enduring industry standard. The new standard effectively gave IBM control of the wider computing environment, and a brand that spelled service, safety and continuity in an uncertain world.

Information systems were, despite their expense, horribly unreliable. Buying the wrong system could be the kiss of death to a corporate career, but no one, it was said, was ever sacked for buying IBM. If an IBM system went wrong, then at least 'Big Blue' had the size and staying power to be around to help.

Few competitors could compete directly with the industry giant, but many smaller players, including minicomputer makers Digital Equipment Corp. and Hewlett-Packard, found unexploited niches where IBM had not yet set a standard. Meanwhile, other smaller entrepreneurial outfits enjoyed symbiotic relationships with Big Blue, developing programs and peripherals to complement IBM's massively profitable product range.

Towards the end of the 1970s a new wave of competitors sprang up, drawn in by IBM's fat margins. The newcomers, led by the Amdahl Corp., built and attempted to market whole computers that were IBM-compatible but were bigger, faster and, above all, cheaper than IBM's own machines. In 1979 IBM suffered its first earnings drop in 28 years, having been forced to cut prices. The Amdahl Corp., being no longer able to undercut IBM to a degree that was sufficient to overcome the fear and perceived risk of a non-IBM purchase, was squeezed to the brink of oblivion. Scorched by the incident, IBM launched itself, and the industry as a whole, with quickened pace on a path towards the development of new basic technologies that would provide greater computing power at lower cost. In doing so the industry was adhering to the maxim of Moore's law, a phenomenon identified in 1965 by Gordon Moore, a founder of the semiconductor manufacturer, Intel Corp. Moore postulated that, measured against price, the performance of semiconductor technology doubles every eighteen months. Slimmer margins demanded higher volumes, so speed of development became more important than ever.

IBM gradually moved to wider market coverage, competing head on in the minicomputer sector, and following others into the growing microcomputer market. However, the falling price of computing power had already conjured up a new breed of competitor: the personal computer makers. IBM hesitated at first but then, in August 1981, plunged into this turbulent new segment with the launch of its Personal Computer – the 'PC'.

The PC was the first computer IBM had produced with a large proportion of components supplied by outsiders. The outsourced components included the core microprocessors and the operating systems that harness their power. IBM had the capabilities to deliver both but, hurrying to get the PC to market, chose instead to outsource them through non-exclusive agreements. The microprocessors came from Intel, and the operating system from an obscure software producer called Microsoft. IBM simply brought the parties together and then, using its legendary marketing capabilities and powerful brand, marketed the product.

The PC was technologically unremarkable but, bearing the IBM logo, it was an immediate success. By 1984 Big Blue held 34 per cent of the exploding personal computer market and 60–70 per cent of the corporate segment. Analysts predicted that the corporate segment would provide the greatest opportunities for growth in forthcoming years, in terms of both hardware sales and service contracts. IBM was riding higher than ever, turning in record profit growth, even by its own exceptional standards. In the eyes of thousands of nervous corporate buyers, the IBM logo on the outside of the PC did more than inspire confidence in IBM's own product; it legitimised the entire personal computer sector.

IBM had originally envisaged that most personal computers would be linked up to its still relatively high margin mainframes, spurring demand for the latter. It realised – too late – that the cheap and increasingly versatile personal computers were gnawing away at its high-end business. Worse still, IBM had maintained its value-added service strategy for mainframes but opted to distribute its PCs through third-party retailers – removing the opportunity to add service value to its technologically undifferentiated product. Big Blue had left the door wide open for low-cost clones using cheaper distribution and direct service provision to undercut the PC. By 1990 hundreds of IBM-clone makers had sprung up to fill the value vacuum, many of them aided and abetted by Microsoft and Intel.

IBM's brand had fostered Microsoft and speeded the growth of Intel, providing a market for their products and imbuing them with the credibility of their host. With that credibility established, the two vital value-added suppliers actively encouraged entrepreneurial new personal computer makers to adopt the latest Microsoft/Intel architectures, undercutting, outpacing, and outperforming IBM.

Recession in the early 1990s made corporate buyers more value conscious and far more willing to shop around. As computing became cheaper, buying decisions were decentralised and pushed down the organisation. Younger corporate buyers with no manufacturer loyalties increasingly viewed hardware as a commodity. The real value lay in services, software, and the new applications created by better basic technology.

By the early 1990s it was Microsoft and Intel, not IBM, who dictated the nature and velocity of competition within the computer industry. A decade later, worldwide, 90 per cent of personal computers sold carried the 'Wintel' combination of Microsoft's Windows software and Intel's Pentium chips.

Intel's iron grip on the high-performance processor market loosened slightly in 2000, following significant performance problems with its newly launched Pentium 4 processors. The lapse allowed long-term competitor Advanced Micro Devices to rush in to fill the resulting vacuum in the high-performance processor market. Nevertheless, having overcome the problem with the Pentium, Intel fought back with massive price cuts, taking as much as 40 per cent off the prices of the rest of its Pentium line. By anyone's reckoning, computer hardware is a commodity.

Concentration of buying power

As we have commented, a significant trend in today's marketing environment is the continuing concentration of buying power. Consolidation has occurred as organisations merge or grow through takeovers, and as the inevitable result of a competitive process that leads to the 'survival of the fittest'.

This process of consolidation seems to be present in just about every industry. The grocery retail market is a very visible example. Figure 1.1 shows the percentage of the total market in Western European economies accounted for by the top three retailers in those countries.

In these same markets pan-European and even global retailers (e.g. Wal-Mart) are emerging, which will add to the concentration effect. These companies seek to use their greater buying power to gain better prices than they might otherwise achieve by acting as single country players.

The process of concentration in other industries in Western Europe has been further accelerated through European economic and monetary integration. Historically countries had tended to develop their own industrial base independently from their neighbours, but as the barriers to trade have fallen significant overcapacity has been revealed. If a comparison is made between the USA and the countries of the European Union – in total the size of their populations are roughly

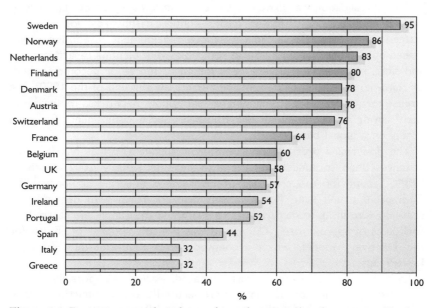

Figure 1.1 Percentage market share of top three retailers by country (*Source*: A. C. Nielsen (2003) *The Shrinking World*)

similar – then it is found that in many cases in comparable industries there have tended to be more players in Europe than in the USA. The 'single market' across the countries of the European Union has led to an increase in cross-border mergers as companies seek economies of scale and rationalisation of capacity.

At the same time that customers are growing in purchasing power, so also are they seeking to do business with fewer suppliers. Many companies have active programmes of supplier rationalisation under way. These companies are looking to their remaining suppliers to take a more proactive role in working more closely at the interface between their organisations to take out cost through such initiatives as vendor-managed inventory (VMI) programmes (see Chapter 5). To become a preferred supplier in this new competitive environment clearly demands competencies and capabilities that go beyond the traditional '4 Ps' marketing mix.

A shrinking supply of suppliers

The 1990s saw the world's motor manufacturers moving one after the other to reduce the size of their supplier bases. The Ford Motor Co., for example, reduced its stable from 10 000 to 2300 during the first half of the decade, declaring its intention in 1996 to reduce the number to 1150 by the decade's end.

The consolidation was driven by the carmakers, who pressed suppliers to provide whole systems for vehicles – entire dashboards, for instance, instead of just the ashtray. Similarly, more development responsibility was placed on suppliers, favouring those companies with plentiful capacity, capital and skills. Many smaller players were forced to merge or become second- or third-tier suppliers to the remaining giants. By the end of the 1990s, the largest carmakers were demanding global supply networks. To maximise their buying power, they looked to single-source components for each model on a global basis.

The downward pressure on component suppliers' prices has in some instances been too much for them to bear. In January 2002, receivers KPMG, acting for the creditors of insolvent engineering company UPF-Thompson, issued Land Rover (a subsidiary of Ford) with demands for around £40m in up-front payments to guarantee the supply of chassis. UPF had debts of approximately £50m, and was the sole supplier of chassis for the Discovery model, which accounted for around one-third of Land Rover's output.

Land Rover's management was outraged. Facing the possibility of a shutdown in production, it immediately secured a court injunction forcing UPF to maintain supply in the short term. Land Rover went on to offer a £4m 'goodwill' payment and a 20 per cent price increase in a bid to stave off the problem long enough for another supplier to acquire the failed UPF.

The receivers had in the meantime issued similar demands to other customers, including manufacturers of Britain's famous black taxis and subsidiaries of Volkswagen and of the world's largest carmaker GM. KPMG justified its actions by pointing out that it was legally obliged to treat a sole customer relationship as a valuable asset that should be exploited for the benefit of creditors. The receiver was following a legal precedent set two years earlier by another insolvent Ford supplier. In that case the judge had ruled that receivers were entitled to exploit the vulnerability of their clients' customers, as their primary responsibility was to pay creditors.

The fragmentation of consumer markets

Paradoxically, whilst buying power in business-to-business markets is tending to concentrate, in consumer markets the trend has been towards fragmentation. Fragmentation here means a transition from the old idea of a uniform, homogeneous 'mass market' to much smaller segments where consumers seek individual solutions to their buying needs. The idea of 'micro-marketing' is an attempt to focus marketing strategies upon ever-smaller groupings of customers. For example, food retailers are now creating merchandising strategies for individual stores based upon the analysis of local geo-demographic statistics and sales patterns from scanner data. In a different market, Dell Computer rose to the top of its sector by virtue of its ability to configure a PC from a range of options and then have the equipment delivered direct to the customer. Dell developed this capability long before the boom in Internet trading and the accompanying renaissance in home shopping.

The aim of micro-marketing is to get as close as possible to the ultimate 'segment of one', whereby tailored solutions for individual customers are put together. Clearly, to get anywhere close to this requires a significant element of flexibility and ever-higher levels of responsiveness on the part of the supplier.

In the fragmented market place the conventional tools of mass marketing no longer have the same effect. National advertising campaigns through the mass media, for example, may no longer be the most cost-effective way of communicating with these micro-markets. At the same time there is evidence that the more sophisticated consumer is influenced less and less by traditional advertising, and that more purchase decisions are actually made at the point of sale.

However, whilst mass media communication may no longer be cost-effective in reaching micro-markets, increasingly sophisticated 'Database Marketing' (DBM) techniques can assist in understanding and communicating with customers who have specific characteristics and attributes. Using data from a variety of sources and powerful computing technology it is possible to zero in on relatively small groups of customers with similar profiles. This enables a highly targeted approach to marketing communications to be effected.

Making use of computerised customer information files that are constructed on a 'relational' basis (i.e. different elements of information can be brought together from separate files) enables the marketer to target more precisely the message to the individual customer or prospective customer.

It is not just computer technology that has made DBM a reality; it is also the rapid growth in the availability of detailed information on individual customers in many markets. A major spur to the use of DBM in consumer markets particularly has come through rapid developments in the field of *geo-demographics*.

Geo-demographics is the generic term applied to the construction of relational databases that draw together data on demographic variables (e.g. age, sex, location), socio-economic variables (e.g. occupation, income), purchase behaviour, lifestyle information, and indeed any data that might usefully describe the characteristics of an individual customer. Much of this information is available through sources such as the Census of Population, electoral rolls, Target Group Index (TGI), National Shoppers' Survey (NSS), credit card purchase data and so on, all of which can be related to postcode areas and, in some cases, to individuals.

Commercially available geo-demographic profiling services, such as Lifestyle View, use a variety of segmentation systems (such as PRIZM or Super Profile) to assist marketers in targeting far more precisely the appropriate audience. For example, it is now possible to identify with a high level of accuracy the characteristics of every one of the UK's 15 million postcodes – each with a maximum of about fifteen addresses.

One of the major opportunities that DBM provides is the facility to profile the organisation's existing customer base and then to seek other potential customers with similar profiles. Similarly, the increasingly detailed information on individuals' purchase behaviour that is now available makes it much easier to target them with appropriate communications for products or services.

DBM also facilitates a much greater degree of personalisation of customer contact. Direct mail can be made more specific to the recipient. Catalogues, newsletters and even magazines can be tailored to the known interests and preferences of the individual. One company in the USA, Donnelly, provides a specialised printing service so that many different versions of a single magazine can be printed with editorial and advertising content tailored to small groups of sub-scribers. One magazine, *Farm Journal*, is printed in 8000 different editions, each one of which goes to a specific segment of readers, according to their demographic profile, farm size, type of crop or livestock, and so on.

Retailers have been amongst the first to recognise the marketing opportunities for building customer loyalty provided by DBM. Customers are encouraged to register for 'frequent shopper' pro-grammes and to benefit from discounts and special promotions if they present their card at the checkout counter when making their purchases. As a result the customer's precise purchase history can be recorded, along with their demographic profile, lifestyle and other details. This enables tailored promotions to be offered, cross-selling to be facilitated and, importantly, the merchandise mix in that store to be matched more precisely to the customers' requirements. As we have already noted, many retail chains are developing specific merchandise and marketing strategies for individual stores so that a store patronised by shoppers with particular demographic profiles and known purchasing preferences will carry a mix of products appro-priate to the customer base.

Tesco Clubcard

In the past decade, there have been three events that have been significant in elevating the status of direct marketing in the UK: Heinz UK's decision to syphon £25m of its ad budget below the line; the appointment of a direct marketer – John Farrell – to the helm of one of the world's top advertising networks; and the launch of Tesco Clubcard.

... It is the launch of Clubcard, however that many believe to be the defining moment in the development and acceptance of database marketing. Not only did the scheme make history – it helped to propel Tesco into the number one slot and left Sainsbury's trailing in its wake – but demonstrated how effective the medium could be, if practised properly.

(Tesco success drives Dunn Humby forward, *Precision Marketing*, 21 September 2001, p. 11)

On 13 February 1995, grocery multiple Tesco launched 'Clubcard', the UK's first national supermarket loyalty scheme. A spokesman for Tesco explained that the principal objective of the scheme was not to lure shoppers away from competitors' stores. He went on to add that Tesco was aiming to recreate the kind of relationship that had existed between local shops and their customers 50 years ago.

Membership of the Clubcard scheme is open to all Tesco customers, through any of its 678 stores. Cards are issued on application. The customer then presents the magnetic stripe card at the checkout, where it is swiped through existing credit-card reading equipment. Details of the purchases are recorded, with Clubcard points automatically awarded for every £1 spent in the store. At the end of each quarter, points are added up and money-off vouchers are mailed to the customers' homes to be redeemed against future spending. The scheme allows customers to claim a 1 per cent discount on their annual shopping bills.

The costs of running the Clubcard scheme are considerable. In addition to the 1 per cent discount to shoppers, Tesco estimated that the start-up costs alone were in the region of £10m. However, the company was convinced that it was money well spent. During pre-launch trials at fourteen stores over 250 000 Clubcards were issued, representing an uptake at the sites involved of between 70 and 80 per cent.

At the time, other leading supermarket chains were expected to follow with their own loyalty card schemes. However, in a statement to the press David Sainsbury, then Chairman of market leader J. Sainsbury, famously dismissed the scheme as a 'Green Shield Stamp way of offering value. We have no plans at all to go down that route'.

Sainsbury's Green Shield Stamp analogy missed an important point. Tesco's multi-million pound investment was actually buying a wealth of self-renewing data on its current customer base. Operational benefits – such as refined stock selection, display and staffing levels – could be derived from the data and were not to be overlooked, but the primary purpose of the data gathering was to facilitate micro-marketing activities. The stream of customer purchase data – what they purchased, how much they spent, when, and how often – revealed a great deal about the lifestyles of shoppers themselves. From this data Tesco could segment its customer base according to real purchase behaviour rather than a version of purchase behaviour based on demographic or socio-economic stereotypes. The data could be used to build loyalty through tailored, value-based offers mailed to homes of specific groups of customers.

By the end of March 1995 over 5 million people had joined the Clubcard scheme, and Tesco's sales had for the first time surged ahead of Sainsbury's – making it Britain's leading retailer of packaged goods.

Within a year Sainsbury's and most of the UK's other leading grocery retailers did introduce their own loyalty card schemes, with varying degrees of success. Many still viewed their card schemes as tactical marketing devices. Some of the cards did have data capture facilities, but the retailers themselves lacked the expertise to handle and exploit the vast amounts of data collected.

Tesco had, however, employed a small specialist data consultancy, Dunn Humby & Associates, to measure what was happening in nine stores during the initial trials for Clubcard. The grocer retained Dunn Humby's services thereafter, to advise it on cost-effective ways to manage and develop the Clubcard database.

As Tesco became more adept at exploiting the database, it was able to extend the range of the Clubcard offers it made to customers. Initially offers had taken the form of money-off vouchers for promoted branded goods, but as the scheme became established these were widened to included discounts on a range of other products and services, such as DIY materials or package holidays, provided by other organisations who were eager to become affiliated to the scheme.

Tesco went on to launch its own charge card, Clubcard Plus, in June 1996, heralding the supermarket's move into the financial services sector. The exploitation of the Internet as a medium for home shopping was seen as the next frontier for the UK grocers. The Clubcard database once more provided essential insights, which by 2001 had enabled Tesco to become the UK's largest 'e-tailer'. With 1 million on-line customers, Tesco was delivering more Internet grocery orders than any other company in the world. By then, though, many of the other UK grocers had abandoned their loyalty card schemes, claiming that the schemes were too expensive to run and that they no longer offered a competitive advantage as customers tended to hold several different retailers' loyalty cards. There was widespread speculation that Clubcard had also had its day. Tesco thought otherwise.

In 2000 Tesco had taken a controlling stake in Dunn Humby, rather than risk losing the expertise the consultancy offered. The retailer had gone on to open up a new revenue stream by selling anonymous customer profile data from its 10 million active Clubcard holders directly to branded goods manufacturers. Furthermore, it was the only retailer in the world able to provide reliable data on how consumer behaviour on-line differs from in-store buying behaviour.

The use of DBM is widespread within the service industries. Frequent-flyer and hotel club schemes have been around for some time, but organisations have progressively become more adept at utilising their potential. Thus not only is the individual's purchase behaviour known, but this can also be correlated with the background information previously collected on that person. Relationships can thus be enhanced because it becomes possible to customise the service – for example, seating and food preferences on an airline or room preferences in a hotel can be easily catered for.

Fast-moving consumer goods (FMCG) companies are increasingly able to pinpoint likely targets for their products through DBM. More importantly, they can use it to strengthen relationships with key customers by designing promotions and incentives that will bind customers more closely to the company. For example, data collected through surveys such as the National Shoppers' Survey (NSS) are available on over 3 million individual customers in the UK, enabling marketers to target heavy users in their product category, or to select users of competitive products for targeted promotions.

In consumer durables, car companies are using DBM to improve customer retention rates. Saab, for example, collects an extensive range of details on each of their customers at the time of buying a car (they up-date the information every six months). Using these data, Saab can design appropriate joint promotions with other companies with a high level of potential appeal to Saab customers – e.g. Bang & Olufsen or Laurent Perrier Champagne. As the time approaches when existing customers are likely to be in the market for a new car, an individually focused marketing programme begins. Clearly if the company knows who the key prospects are it can afford to spend a lot more on sales and marketing per individual, in the knowledge that the sales and marketing effort will be much more effective because it is specific to a particular person.

In business-to-business marketing there has been a recent upsurge of interest in Customer Relationship Management (CRM), which builds on the platform that DBM provides. CRM can be defined as:

> ... A strategic approach to improving shareholder value through the development of appropriate relationships with key customers and customer segments. CRM unites the potential of IT and relationship marketing strategies to deliver profitable, long-term relationships. Importantly, CRM provides enhanced opportunities to use data and information both to understand customers and implement relationship marketing strategies better. This requires a cross-functional integration of people, operations and marketing capabilities enabled through information technology and applications.
>
> (Christopher, Payne and Ballantyne (2002)
> *Relationship Marketing*, 2nd edn. Butterworth-Heinemann)

Powerful software packages are now available that enable organisations to be far more focused in the way in which they create and deliver service solutions for individual customers. In effect, we are seeing a transition from 'mass marketing' to 'one-to-one marketing'. Thus database marketing is transforming the ways in which fragmented markets can be addressed and individualised communications delivered. Combine this with flexibility of response in terms of the design and delivery of products or services, and a significant competitive opportunity emerges.

The service-sensitive customer

It has now become an accepted fact of commercial life that customer service is a critical determinant in winning and keeping customers.

Today's customer in virtually every market is demanding ever-higher levels of performance from suppliers, particularly in respect to delivery service. In many organisations the focus upon inventory reduction has caused them to look closely at the quality of the in-bound delivery service they receive from suppliers. At the other end of the marketing channel, consumers have become equally demanding in their service requirements. In the era of fast food and convenience stores, there is less willingness to wait. Various surveys have suggested that up to two-thirds of all shopping decisions in a supermarket are now taken at the point of purchase. As a result, on-the-shelf availability will often overcome brand preference.

The challenge to the organisation that aspires to be a leader in service performance is to recognise the service requirements of the different segments that it serves and to restructure its logistics processes around the achievement of those service requirements.

Organisations in virtually every market sector have come to recognise that differentiation through superior customer service offers an opportunity to avoid price competition. Whilst there will always be 'price buyers' in any market, there are also large numbers of service-sensitive customers. The success of companies such as Marks & Spencer in selling, at relatively high prices, oven-ready gourmet-style meals demonstrated that there are significant numbers of customers who are 'time-sensitive' rather than 'price-sensitive'. In a different market, RS Components, an electronic parts distributor, has been able to maintain above-average margins as a result of above-average service.

RS Components

Based in Corby, Northamptonshire, RS Components is widely regarded as a service leader in its field. Many of the items it supplies are critical to the operation of customer's equipment. Consequently, customers are prepared to pay a considerable premium for these items in order to obtain rapid response and certainty of supply.

RS guarantees next-day delivery almost anywhere in the UK for any of the 130 000 items listed in its catalogue. Items can be ordered on-line, by fax or by telephone. Delivery is free of charge for credit account holders, though surcharges are levied for very urgent time-guaranteed deliveries. For these RS operates a sliding scale of charges, which in 2002 ranged from £15 for delivery before 9.00 am the next day, to £9 for delivery before noon.

RS's reputation for service excellence and convenience has allowed it to expand its business in recent years from electrical/electronic components into a whole range of other complementary product categories, including tools, health and safety products, office equipment and books.

The sources of marketing advantage

In the new competitive environment, it is increasingly evident that successful marketing strategies are based upon an amalgam of three critical elements. The first is the creation of a portfolio of *innovative products* that can solve real problems and deliver recognisable and relevant benefits to customers. Underpinning the offer should be a strong *brand* appeal, be it a corporate image or individual product. Secondly, there should be a strong *customer relationship* so that intermediaries want to do business with the company because of a tangible economic benefit; thirdly, there should be an underpinning *supply chain effectiveness* that delivers superior service at less cost. Figure 1.2 summarises the three sources of competitive advantage.

Figure 1.2 The sources of marketing advantage

Each of the three dimensions requires a clearly defined strategy, but should be developed as part of an integrative package to deliver superior value to customers and consumers alike.

Innovation and branding

Whilst brand loyalty may no longer be as strong as it once was, the need to build a 'contract' with the end-user is still a vital prerequisite for marketing advantage. Brand value is still a critical element in many purchase decisions, although it seems that there has been a return to a

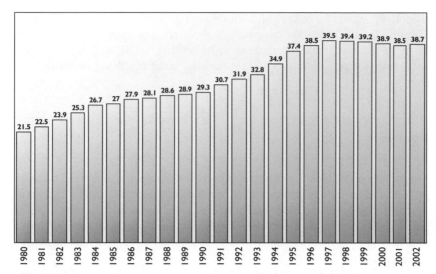

Figure 1.3 Own-label share of trade (PL% packaged grocery – long-term trends): 1977–1999 (*Source*: Taylor Nelson Sofres Superpanel)

concept of value based upon traditional tangible or 'core' benefits rather than the more emotionally-based, intangible benefits that appear to have fixated many marketers in the last quarter-century. Now it seems that consumer loyalty is more often based upon 'hard' rather than 'soft' dimensions, and so value for money, convenience, reliability, safety and functionality become the drivers of product or service choice. The impact of own-label, retailer-branded products in many categories is further testimony to this development. Coca-Cola, regarded as the world's most recognised brand, has seen its market share in the USA and the UK (and elsewhere too) eroded by own-label products that are seen by customers to deliver better value for money. Figure 1.3 shows the growing penetration of own-label products in the UK packaged grocery market.

What this means for twenty-first century marketers is that in order to strengthen the consumer franchise, the focus of marketing effort must increasingly be upon delivering 'solutions' that can be translated into hard, tangible benefits for individual consumers. In many cases this will further hasten the transition to 'micro' or 'one-to-one' marketing, whereby a greater degree of tailoring/customisation of the product offer is achieved.

It also implies that an even greater emphasis must be placed on innovation. In a crowded market place the consumer is surrounded by 'look-alikes' and 'me-too's'. When products are introduced that provide significant benefits to consumers, they will often sell in significant volumes, at higher prices. In the fiercely competitive 'laundry' market (soaps and detergents), Unilever and Procter & Gamble battle more on innovation than they do on the TV screen. Time-to-market becomes increasingly critical, facilitated by a corporate culture that encourages risk-taking and thinking 'outside the box'.

Soap wars

In February 2001 McBride, a small own-label consumer goods manufacturer, pulled off one of the greatest new product development coups in recent years. In doing so, McBride demonstrated that an own-label manufacturer could not only compete with the largest branded goods makers on price and product quality; it also had the capability to outperform them in product innovation.

The laundry detergent market is amongst the most mature of all consumer goods categories – demand is flat, and growth is non-existent. In Western Europe, marketers representing Unilever's Persil brand and Procter & Gamble's Ariel have been engaged for decades in the commercial equivalent of trench warfare. The global giants' brands are firmly entrenched, not least because household laundry brand preferences tend to be passed on from one generation to the next. Despite billions of dollars of marketing spend, only true value-adding innovations have had a marked impact on the *status quo*.

It is widely recognised that consumers are most likely to switch brands in the time between an innovative new product reaching the shelves and the inevitable arrival of their usual brand's 'me-too' offer. Retailers' own-label products, each accounting for only a tiny proportion of the overall market, were invariably 'me-too's', and consequently had been viewed almost as an irrelevance by the two big multinationals.

In the UK the nimbler Unilever's Persil brand had been the market leader for decades, until in 1994 its eagerness to gain first-mover advantage with a radical new formula drove it to launch 'Persil Power'. The product was launched with insufficient testing. P&G went on to demonstrate how Persil Power's 'accelerator' could damage customers' clothing, and sales of Ariel surged past Persil. In a determined bid to retain its lead, P&G quickly began a dramatic restructuring of its worldwide operations to reduce time-to-market for innovative new products.

At the time, the mainstream laundry detergents market fell into two broad, stable categories – powder and liquid – with customers loyal to one or other delivery form. Some buyers preferred powder because of its supposed greater cleaning ability; others preferred liquid because it left less residue on the clothes. Persil and Ariel were available in both forms. In purely performance terms laundry detergents had reached something of a functional plateau, with further marginal improvements unlikely to lure customers away from competitors' brands.

In 1998 Unilever did manage to claw back its lost share when it beat P&G to market with the introduction of Persil Tablets, a compact and convenient ready-measured alternative to powder. Persil managed to hold on to its gain, despite P&G's rapid response with Ariel Tablets.

Having identified convenience as a source of value-adding product differentiation, both major manufacturers knew that pre-measured portions for liquid detergent buyers was the obvious next step in product innovation.

On 15 February 2001, a buzz of excitement went through the marketing press. Big-budget advertising campaigns were being prepared for Unilever and P&G. However, the flurry of excitement centred on the news that Unilever's hopes of being first to market with 'Persil Capsules' were about to be dashed. Unilever was ramping up for a launch in April, but P&G had announced its intention to launch 'Ariel Liqui-Tabs' in March. On 19 February, one of Britain's smaller grocery multiples, the Co-operative Group, stunned the world by announcing that within the week it would be introducing 'Brio Actipods'. McBride, its small own-label manufacturer, had beaten all comers in the race to bring liquid detergent capsules to market.

Customer relationships

As the power of intermediaries has strengthened in many markets, it is of paramount importance to make the customer – not just the consumer – an integral part of marketing strategy. Whether an intermediary is a retailer, a distributor or an original equipment manufacturer (OEM), without its support it is unlikely that even the strongest brand could achieve its full potential.

Not only has the purchasing power of the customer increased as a result of concentration, but also, as we suggested earlier, there is a growing trend towards 'single-sourcing' by those customers. In other words, whereas in the past the practice was to spread the total purchase of an item across several suppliers, now the aim is to reduce the size of the supplier base and to seek further cost reductions as a result.

Whilst to many suppliers such developments may be perceived as a threat, to others they present an opportunity. If the supplier can offer a superior value package with a measurable positive economic impact on the customer, then the likelihood is that it will win the business. Today's customer is a more sophisticated buyer, used to working with concepts such as total cost of ownership, life-cycle costing and cost–benefit analysis. Indeed many customers now actively pursue a 'partnership sourcing' strategy, whereby they seek to establish long-term relationships with preferred suppliers based upon 'win–win' philosophies.

Supply chain effectiveness

In the new market place there is a strong case for arguing that individual companies no longer compete with other stand-alone companies, but rather that supply chain now competes against supply chain. The rationale for this viewpoint is based upon the fact that when organisations work independently of their upstream suppliers and downstream customers, costs and inefficiencies tend to build up at the interfaces.

Supply chain management can be defined as 'the management of upstream and downstream relationships with suppliers, distributors and customers to achieve greater customer value at less cost'.

Formalised supply chain management is increasingly being recognised as a critical determinant of competitive advantage. Because both total costs and customer service are heavily impacted by the structure of the supply chain and the effectiveness of its co-ordination, it is essential that a greater emphasis be placed upon its management.

The need for co-ordination between partners in the supply chain has increased as the 'network organisation' becomes more common. The network organisation comprises a complex web of linkages between focused partners, each of which adds value through specialisation in an activity where it can achieve a differential advantage.

This progress towards the idea of supply chain integration as a source of competitive advantage will gain momentum as the growth of 'time-based competition' accelerates. In markets that are increasingly volatile, responsiveness becomes a critical competitive requirement. In the apparel industry, companies like Benetton and Zara have gained significant advantage through their ability to respond rapidly to fashion changes in the markets that they serve. Through the use of highly co-ordinated logistics and supply chain structures, driven by the real-time capture of sales data, these companies and others like them can adapt their product range and their volumes in weeks rather than months.

Later in this book examples will be given of organisations that have significantly enhanced their competitive performance by focusing upon improving both upstream and downstream linkages with their supply chain partners. What will be apparent is that this concept of supply chain integration requires a fundamentally different approach to relationships within the marketing channel. Traditional buyer–supplier relationships, which have tended towards the adversarial, need to be reassessed and be replaced with a philosophy of co-operation and 'win–win' thinking.

The new market place: key issues

- ■ The changing nature of the market place
  - ● Customer and consumer sophistication
  - ● Erosion of brand loyalty
  - ● Downward pressure on price

- ■ The growth in customer power
  - ● Concentration of buyer power
  - ● Customers rationalising the supplier base
  - ● Demise of the mass market

- ■ The focus on 'micro-markets'
  - ● The advent of database marketing
  - ● The importance of geo-demographics
  - ● Better target marketing

- ■ The sources of marketing advantage
  - ● Innovation and branding
  - ● Customer relationships
  - ● Supply chain effectiveness

Chapter 2

Building customer relationships

As markets mature and the cost of winning new customers steadily increases, greater emphasis needs to be placed upon retaining existing customers and building the business that is done with them. Market share, which for long was the overriding goal of many corporations, is being replaced by a focus on *customer share* – in other words, what share of the customer's spending are we getting, and what is the *quality* of that share (i.e. how loyal are those customers?). Much evidence exists to suggest that retained customers are generally more profitable than new ones, and hence the marketing challenge is to find ways of building enduring relationships with selected customers. Whilst many factors will influence the quality and longevity of a customer relationship, it will usually be the case that superior service performance will be a key determinant of customer retention.

Customer retention strategies

It has been suggested that it costs up to five times as much to win a new customer as it does to retain an existing one. The costs of capturing market share are not always easy to gauge, but there are many companies now that regret earlier strategies that were based upon the blind pursuit of volume. Whilst there is strong evidence for the link between market share and profitability, there is equally strong evidence to show that it is the *quality* of that market share that counts. In other words, does our customer base comprise, in the main, long-established, loyal customers, or is there a high degree of turnover or 'churn'? If the latter is the case, then the chances are that we are not as profitable as we might be.

Bain & Company, the international consulting company, has suggested that even a relatively small improvement in the customer retention rate (measured as the percentage of retained business from one period to another) can have a marked impact upon profitability. They suggest that on average, an improvement of 5 percentage points in customer retention can lead to profit improvements of between 25 and 85 per cent in the net present value of the future flow of earnings.

Why should a retained customer be more profitable than a new one? First, because of the costs of acquiring new business in the first place, it might take time to bring new customers into profit. Secondly, the more satisfied customers are with the relationship, the more likely they are to place a bigger proportion of their total purchase with us, even to the extent of 'single sourcing' from us. Thirdly, these retained customers become easier to sell to, with consequent lower costs; they are also more likely to be willing to integrate their systems (e.g. their planning, scheduling and ordering systems) with ours, leading to further cost reductions. In some markets satisfied customers may also refer others to us, leading to a further enhancement of profitability. Finally, Bain & Company suggested that loyal customers were often less price-sensitive and would be less inclined to switch suppliers because of price rises.

All of these elements together combine to lead to the conclusion that retained customers can generate considerably more profit than new ones. Figure 2.1 summarises this relationship.

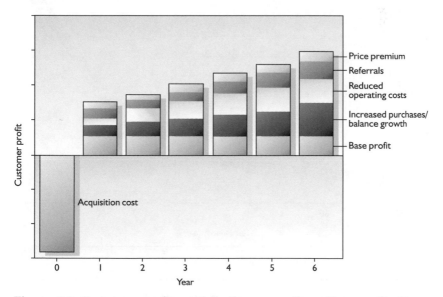

Figure 2.1 Customer profit contribution over time (*Source***: Customer retention model, Bain & Company 1996)**

A study in the North American car industry suggested that a satisfied customer is likely to stay with the same supplier for a further twelve years after the first satisfactory purchase, and during that period will buy four more cars of the same make. It is estimated that, to a car manufacturer, this level of customer retention is worth $400 million in new car sales annually.

There is a direct linkage between the customer retention rate and the average lifetime of a customer. For example, if the customer retention rate is 90 per cent per annum (meaning a loss of 10 per cent of the existing customer base each year) then the average customer lifetime will be ten years. If, on the other hand, the retention rate can be improved to 95 per cent per annum (a loss of 5 per cent of the customer base each year) then the average customer life will be twenty years – in other words, a doubling of the average customer life is achieved for a relatively small improvement in the retention rate. Figure 2.2 illustrates the relationship between the retention rate and the customer lifetime.

An important statistic that is not always measured is the *lifetime value of a customer*. Put very simply, this is a measure of the financial worth to the organisation of a retained customer. If customers are loyal and continue to spend money with the company into the future, then clearly their lifetime value is greater than that of a customer who buys only once or twice then switches to another brand or supplier.

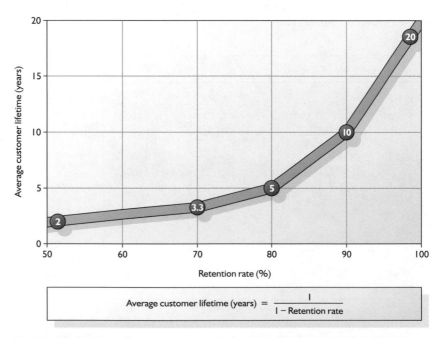

Figure 2.2 **Impact of customer retention rate on customer lifetime** (*Source*: Bain & Company 1996)

Measuring the lifetime value of a customer requires an estimation of the likely cash flow to be provided if that customer were to achieve an average loyalty level. In other words, if a typical account lasts for ten years then we would need to calculate the net present value of the profits that would flow from that customer over ten years. We are now in a position to calculate the impact that increasing the retention rate of customers would have upon profitability and also what the effect of extending the customer lifetime by a given amount would be. This information provides a good basis for marketing investment decision-making – in other words, how much is it worth spending, either to improve the retention rate or to extend the life of a customer?

Understanding the reasons for customer 'defection' can help in developing customer retention strategies. Why do customers leave? Surprisingly, few companies carry out formal follow-up research amongst lapsed customers. There are many reasons why customers depart, but normally the 80/20 rule will be evident – that is, 80 per cent of customers leave for the same 20 per cent of reasons. The purpose of customer defection research is to get at the root causes of customer loss.

Research into lost customers should be carried out through in-depth interviews with decision makers. The objective of this research is to dig as deeply as possible below the surface to identify the real reasons for defection. For instance, many customers may cite 'price' as the reason for leaving, but that might simply be a 'top of the head' response and there may well be underlying reasons to do with customer service, lack of responsiveness, unreliability and so on. As decisions to change suppliers or brands are not taken lightly by most customers, it will usually be cumulative dissatisfaction that triggers the decisions. It follows therefore that if the causes of dissatisfaction can be pinned down, actions can be taken to remove them.

Often customer complaints will provide an indication of the cause of dissatisfaction, but it must be remembered that only a minority of customers complain; the rest just vote with their feet. There is something to be said for actively seeking criticism from customers. Regular feedback through formal questionnaires and focus groups is a prerequisite for a continuous programme of improvement in customer relations.

Whilst it has long been acknowledged that the fundamental purpose of marketing is the 'getting and keeping of customers', the truth is that more attention has been paid, typically, to the getting of customers rather than the keeping of them. More recently there has emerged a recognition that marketing needs not only to encompass those activities necessary to capture business in the first place, but also to develop processes that will enhance long-term customer loyalty. This viewpoint is the foundation for the development of the concept of *relationship marketing*, at the heart of which lies the proposition that the

Table 2.1 The shift to relationship marketing

Transactional focus	Relationship focus
Orientation to single sales	Orientation to customer retention
Discontinuous customer contact	Continuous customer contact
Focus on product features	Focus on customer value
Short timescale	Long timescale
Little emphasis on customer service	High customer service emphasis
Quality is the concern of production staff	Quality is the concern of all staff

fundamental purpose of marketing is the creation and development of long-term profitable relationships with customers.

It should not be thought that relationship marketing is a replacement for marketing as it has been practised to date. Rather it is an augmentation and refocusing of the marketing concept with the emphasis placed upon strategies to enhance customer retention and loyalty. Some of the major differences in emphasis between the traditional approach (which we label 'transactional') and the 'relationship' focus are shown in Table 2.1.

It can be seen from Table 2.1 that the major difference between the relationship focus and the transactional focus is the emphasis upon continuous commitment to meeting the needs of individual customers, and that service and quality are particularly stressed.

Many marketing practitioners might justifiably protest that they have been practising relationship marketing for years but did not realise it! In truth, however, many others have failed to recognise the importance of customer loyalty as a driver of profitability and hence have tended to concentrate their effort on a single-minded pursuit of market share.

Relationship marketing as a philosophy is concerned with the 'quality' of market share, not just its absolute level – in other words, the minimisation of customer defections and the building of long-term partnerships with customers who willingly repeat purchase from us.

Relationships as partnerships

The basic philosophy underlying relationship marketing is that the goal of all marketing activity should be the establishment of mutually beneficial partnerships with customers. If customers perceive that there is greater value in staying with a particular supplier than with moving to any other, then clearly they will stay. Hence the challenge to management is to develop marketing strategies that are designed to create enduring customer partnerships.

For example, many companies are benefiting from closer relationships with suppliers. What they are discovering is that by working alongside suppliers they can find ways to take costs out of the supply chain by focusing on such things as just-in-time delivery systems, linking ordering procedures through Electronic Data Interchange (EDI), and eliminating the need for re-work by quality improvement programmes. In addition they can build customer value by working together on product improvements and new product development. Indeed, some studies suggest that a major source of innovation is increasingly the upstream supplier.

Emerging from this concept of partnership is the idea of the 'extended enterprise'. Whilst traditionally companies have tended to see their strengths in terms of their own capabilities and resources, this notion of the 'extended enterprise' looks beyond the legal boundaries of the company for sources of competitive advantage. If the organisations concerned adopt a long-term perspective, then the result of this kind of arrangement – and indeed any successful supply chain management programme – should be enhanced profit for all the partners in the chain.

The concept of the extended enterprise will be discussed further in Chapter 6, but a good example of how an extended enterprise can enable rapid response to changing market requirements is highlighted here – getting the prawn sandwich to market.

Getting the prawn sandwich to market

Gunstones Bakery, a subsidiary of the UK food manufacturer Northern Foods, is one of a small handful of major suppliers of sandwiches to Marks & Spencer (M&S). M&S is Britain's biggest retailer of ready-packed sandwiches, selling between 1 and 2 million units a week.

Owing to the demand for freshness, each sandwich has a maximum shelf life of 48 hours from time of manufacture to point of sale; however, demand is uncertain since one of the biggest determinants of consumption patterns is the weather! The problem is further compounded by the fact that M&S offers 40 different fillings on eight types of bread. Hence the need for a highly integrated supply chain capable of responding rapidly to ensure that the right product is in the right place at the right time.

The very close working relationship between Gunstones Bakery and M&S means they are able to achieve an almost seamless flow of sandwiches into the retailer's 290 stores across Britain. The process begins when M&S places a provisional order mid-week for the following week. This forecast is based on the previous week's sales by store, and is only approximate because of the influence of weather upon demand. On a Friday a second forecast is issued by M&S, which is used by Gunstones to plan their labour requirement for the following week. Gunstones uses permanent labour, with contracts that have built-in flexibility regarding hours of work.

The final order only arrives from M&S at 6 am on the day of manufacture, but the retailer reserves the right to change the order at any time up to 9 am on that day. On occasion it may change the order up to 12 noon, particularly with sudden changes in the weather or if problems arise with M&S's other sandwich suppliers.

Sandwich manufacture at Gunstones begins at 7 am, with the first dispatch to the third-party operated chilled distribution centres beginning at 11.30 am and the last at 8.30 pm. The sandwiches are packed by Gunstones into trays according to type to enable them to be sorted for store delivery at one of several regional distribution centres. The sandwiches will arrive at the stores by 7 am the following day. So an order placed on Thursday is made on Thursday to be in the shops on Friday morning.

Clearly such a responsive logistics system requires close collaboration, not just between M&S and Gunstones but also between Gunstones and its suppliers. Whilst Gunstones bakes its own bread and rolls for the sandwiches, and can freeze and unfreeze loaves depending upon demand, their biggest challenge is managing the supply of fresh produce and short shelf-life items such as lettuce. In fact Gunstones maintains hourly contact with its suppliers of short shelf-life products, and shares with them the latest forecasts from M&S.

The key to the effectiveness of the sandwich supply chain is the high level of communication and shared information between all parties in the chain. For example, Gunstones' senior management will be in constant contact with the M&S opposite numbers. Visits to one another's premises are made frequently. Gunstones also seeks constantly to innovate with new sandwich products and manufacturing processes, and in so doing will work closely with both M&S marketing personnel and the produce suppliers.

Why partner?

In the past, business organisations tended to perform most activities in house. In the era of vertical integration, companies would seek to control through ownership of their entire value chain. Henry Ford I typified this concept – at one time Ford owned a power plant, a steel mill, a glass factory and a rubber factory, as well as mahogany forests. Today, thinking has undergone a 180-degree change, with corporations seeking to focus on core competencies and outsource everything else. By definition, the more companies focus on those activities they believe they have a differential advantage in, the more they need to rely on others. As these external dependencies increase, it becomes vital that the nature of the relationship switches from the arm's-length transactional mode to a collaborative partnership mode.

We would argue that there are three critical capabilities to which any firm must have access:

1 Customer relationship management
2 Innovation
3 Supply chain management.

The business itself may lack the competencies and skills to master all of these, and will almost certainly need to rely upon others to provide some (or all) of the key elements of these processes. The danger in outsourcing anything is the potential for loss of control. In fact, outsourced activities must be even more closely managed than if they were performed in house. The maxim must be, outsource the *execution* of a process but never the *control* of that process. It could be argued that rather than talking about outsourcing we should be using the word 'insourcing' instead. 'Outsourcing' implies putting something *outside* the business (as in subcontracting), whereas 'insourcing' suggests bringing a strength *into* the business – a strength we don't currently have.

It is this realisation – that the organisation no longer stands alone – that is prompting a new search for collaborative partnering. These partnerships may be with suppliers, distributors, retailers, specialist service providers, technology-sharing alliances and, increasingly, with competitors.

The lines between suppliers, customers and competitors are sometimes becoming increasingly blurred. For example, Dell and IBM compete in the PC market, but IBM is also a supplier to Dell (as well as providing components it also has a technology sharing agreement), and it has even been suggested that before long Dell might undertake certain assembly tasks for IBM!

This is a phenomenon that has been called by some 'co-opetition' – i.e. collaborate to compete. The principle that underpins co-opetition is that it may well benefit organisations to collaborate in order to 'grow the pie' but to compete regarding how to slice it. In many retail environments manufacturers of branded products compete with the retailers' own-label products, yet the smart players in those markets have come to recognise the benefits of joint category planning in order to grow total demand within that category. Category management will be dealt with in more detail in Chapter 6.

In competing as a network it becomes apparent that the aim should be to maximise *collaborative advantage* rather than competitive advantage in its traditional, single-firm meaning. To release this collaborative advantage and leverage the collective competitiveness and skills across the network means that knowledge must be shared and harnessed.

'Knowledge management' is the descriptor that is tending to be used as we attempt to develop partnership-based marketing and logistics strategies. The idea behind knowledge management is that:

competencies + skills = capabilities

and that capabilities are what provide competitive advantage. The three key capabilities, it will be recalled, are:

1 Customer relationship management
2 Innovation
3 Supply chain management.

Thus the challenge is to assemble an appropriate set of competencies and skills across these three arenas, and hence the critical importance of partnerships.

Managing relationships in the marketing channel

The old idea that buyers and sellers should maintain a distance from each other and only concern themselves with 'negotiating a deal' can no longer be sustained. Instead the trend is increasingly towards a much wider business-development focused relationship, where the supplier takes a holistic view of the customer's needs. A good example of this is provided by recent developments in what is sometimes termed 'trade marketing'. Whilst much of the emphasis in traditional branded consumer goods marketing has been placed upon end-users to 'pull' the product through the marketing channel, trade marketing is concerned with gaining and retaining access to the marketing channel, thus increasing end-users' 'opportunities to buy' – in other words, ensuring that maximum shelf space, distribution and avail-ability are achieved. Occasionally these strategies are referred to as 'push' strategies; however, such a term implies a production orienta-tion, and it is probably better to talk simply in terms of a 'relationship strategy'.

Figure 2.3 highlights the difference between the two approaches. The conventional buyer–supplier interface, shown in Figure 2.3(a), is a fragile connection, easily broken by competitors, based upon a motivation on the part of the buyer to maximise the margin and on the part of the seller to maximise volume.

In the relationship-based approach, shown in Figure 2.3(b), the two 'triangles' are inverted to bring about a much stronger interface bond. Now there are multiple points of connection between the vendor and the customer. The objectives of the vendor are to develop the

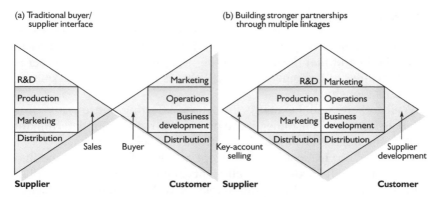

(a) Traditional buyer/supplier interface

(b) Building stronger partnerships through multiple linkages

Figure 2.3 The transition to relationship marketing

customer's business, to focus on the customer's return on investment, and to enhance the customer's own competitive capability. The benefit to the vendor if those objectives are achieved is the likelihood that it will be treated as a preferred supplier. At the same time, the costs of serving that customer should be lower as a result of a greater sharing of information, integrated logistics systems and so on.

To achieve such multiple 'connections' between the two parties clearly requires a mutual understanding of the benefits that can be achieved though partnership. In reality it will require a proactive approach from the vendor in which business solutions are presented to the customer, rather than a sales proposition. For example, many manufacturers marketing to the retail trade now seek to illustrate the impact of a proposed relationship in terms of return on investment within the category in which the product in question competes. Thus the supplier must be able to demonstrate the impact that the relationship can have upon shelf-space profitability, stock-turn and so on.

This new-style partnership approach to channel management challenges much of the conventional thinking about buyer–supplier relationships. It also suggests a more proactive approach to the management of customers – indeed, in a growing number of businesses *customer management* has become a key focus of attention.

Recognising that customer management needs some formal framework upon which to build the relationship, many companies now have formal service level agreements with their customers. The essence of these agreements is that they are negotiated and agreed between the parties, and they set the expectation against which subsequent performance will be managed. Increasingly these agreements will go beyond simple issues of delivery lead times and reliability to encompass wider areas for collaboration.

Defining customer service

Given that customer retention is often a key determinant of long-run profitability and that the quality of the relationship with a customer is clearly related to customer retention, what is it that drives the quality of the relationship?

Whilst there will be many influences affecting the quality of a relationship with a customer, it can be argued that a major determinant will be the degree of satisfaction with the service received.

Customer service is a broad concept and is not easy to define in a single sentence. It encompasses all points of contact between a supplier and a buyer, and includes intangible as well as tangible elements. Logistics performance is clearly a critical dimension in achieving customer satisfaction, and underpins the model of the service–relationship–retention linkage as shown in Figure 2.4.

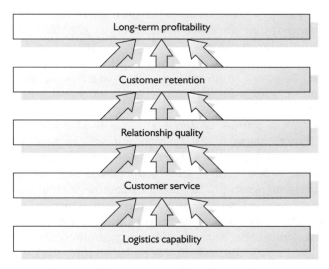

Figure 2.4 Key drivers of long-term profitability

What this model implies is that successful differentiation through customer service requires more than the obvious focus on 'customer care' and 'putting people first' – important though these are. A critical requirement for an organisation seeking to become a service leader in its field is to have a detailed, objective understanding of how customers themselves define service. Once that understanding exists, then strategies can be devised and systems developed to meet (or preferably to exceed) customers' expectations.

The argument advanced here is that organisations need to redefine service in terms that have relevance to customers – indeed, to use the customers' own definitions of service – and to re-engineer logistics processes so that they are geared to the achievement of those service goals.

The components of customer service

There are three elements of customer service:

1 *Pre-transaction elements*. These include:
   - Written customer service policy – is it communicated internally and externally, is it understood, is it specific and quantified where possible?
   - Accessibility – are we easy to contact/do business with? Is there a single point of contact?
   - Organisation structure – is there a customer service management structure in place? What level of control do they have over their service process?
   - System flexibility – can we adapt our service delivery systems to meet particular customer needs?
2 *Transaction elements*. These include:
   - Order cycle time – what is the elapsed time from order to delivery? What is the reliability/variation?
   - Inventory availability – what percentage of demand for each item can be met from stock?
   - Order fill rate – what proportion of orders are completely filled within the stated lead time?
   - Order status information – how long does it take us to respond to a query with the required information? Do we inform the customer of problems or do they contact us?
3 *Post-transaction elements*. These include:
   - Availability of spares – what are the in-stock levels of service parts?
   - Call-out time – how long does it take for the engineer to arrive, and what is the 'first call fix rate'?
   - Product tracing/warranty – can we identify the location of individual products once purchased? Can we maintain/extend the warranty to customers' expected levels?
   - Customer complaints, claims etc. – how promptly do we deal with complaints and returns? Do we measure customer satisfaction with our response?

Traditionally, most measures and standards of customer service are internally focused – in other words, they measure dimensions such as stock availability at a Stock-Keeping Unit (SKU) level, inventory cover expressed in terms of number of days' sales, percentage of lines available for shipment and so on. Furthermore, the conventional approach to customer service strategy has been based upon the concept of 'trade-offs' to achieve so-called optimal levels of service. In this model all the costs of service provision (e.g. inventory, warehousing, transportation, etc.) are totalled and balanced against the cost of a stock-out. The inevitable conclusion of such an exercise in any market is that the ideal level of service is likely to be less than 100 per cent.

An alternative approach, which is much more in accord with today's focus on total quality, is the idea that the goal of any organisation should be to meet 'the service promise' 100 per cent of the time. The service promise is a negotiated service agreement whereby suppliers and customers agree the basis upon which they will trade. It will be a different promise for different customers – not everyone will be promised overnight delivery, for example – and the agreement will be based upon a clear knowledge by the supplier of individual customer profitability.

In any purchase situation it is unlikely that there will be more than three or four really critical service issues from a customer's point of view, and these may be thought of as the 'order winning' criteria and the 'customer retaining' criteria. In other words, these are the elements that the supplying organisation must set out to excel in at each and every customer encounter. Clearly it is essential that the company researches the customer to identify the nature of these criteria and the relative importance attached to them by individual customers.

Not only can this information provide focus for the organisation's customer service strategy, it can also provide the basis for successful market segmentation based upon distinctive service requirements. In other words, instead of offering uniform service packages to all customers, the flexible organisation will seek to differentiate the service packages to meet more closely customers' specific requirements.

Researching the customers' service needs

So many companies assume that they understand their customers and so do not recognise the need for detailed, in-depth research amongst existing and potential customers to identify the critical success factors when it comes to winning and keeping business. All definitions of service should be customer-generated, and the measurement of service performance should be against customer-relevant metrics.

The following five-step approach is recommended as the basis for establishing a meaningful understanding of customers' service needs, and for determining the way those needs may differ by market segments.

1 *Define the competitive arena.* With whom do we compete in the customer's mind? Often customers compare our performance not so much to other direct 'head-to-head' competitors, but rather with other suppliers with whom they do business. Who are the 'best in class', as seen by customers? These are our real competitors.

2 *Understand the dimensions of service.* Customers are the only ones who can articulate the issues that concern them – hence the importance of using research to elicit the dimensions of service as seen by customers, rather than using our own internal definitions of service. Group interviews or focus groups, as well as in-depth interviews, can provide the basis for an objective determination of the dimensions of service.

3 *Identify the key service issues.* Whilst the previous step may have identified multiple issues, the key question is: what are the 'order winning' and 'customer keeping' criteria? In other words, what are the three or four key dimensions that are critical to the customer's choice of supplier? Research techniques such as trade-off analysis can help to quantify the relative importance that customers attach to the different dimensions of service.

4 *Recognise the segmentation of the market.* It is likely that the research undertaken in Step 3 will reveal that different customers attach different levels of importance to the dimensions of service – in other words, not everybody shares the same service priorities. What will often be the case, however, is that clusters or groups of customers will emerge who share similar views on what the key issues are. The clusters may well provide the basis for a redefinition of the market on the basis of service preferences.

5 *Measure performance against best in class.* Using the key service issues, segment by segment, we are now in a position to measure performance against those companies identified by customers in Step 1 as being best in class. Such companies provide a meaningful benchmark and the basis for the delivery of superior service performance.

Such an approach clearly requires a detailed understanding of customers' needs, as well as the value they place upon each element of service. It also requires a level of flexibility throughout the organisation to deliver such packages. Adopting this revised model also requires a rethink on how service performance is measured.

The achievement of the service promise on each and every occasion has been termed the 'perfect order'. The attainment of the perfect order means that each element of the service package has been performed as agreed. One common definition of the perfect order is 'delivered on time, complete and error free'. 'On-time delivery' is measured against the agreed lead time, 'completeness' is measured by 'order fill', and 'error free' includes the avoidance of error in documentation such as invoices, as well as other sources of quality failure in the order fulfilment process.

Table 2.2 Calculation of the perfect order achievement

Order	1	2	3	4	5	6	Total (%)
On time	Y	Y	N	N	Y	N	50
Complete	Y	N	Y	N	Y	N	50
No error	Y	N	Y	Y	Y	N	66
Perfect order	Y	N	N	N	Y	N	33

This is quite a challenging measure for even the best-run organisations. It must be realised that the overall level of service performance during a period is determined by the *combined* effect of each separate element of the perfect order.

The calculation of the perfect order achievement is demonstrated in Table 2.2, where the three key service elements have been identified as on-time delivery, completeness, and no invoice error.

In this case all three elements were only achieved simultaneously on two out of the six orders, and hence on this basis the perfect order achievement is only 33 per cent.

Creating a customer service index

Using the three or four critical service elements, which may differ by customer or market segment or distribution channel, a continuous monitoring process should be established based around the concept of the 'perfect order'. The perfect order is achieved when all the critical service goals are met to the customer's satisfaction.

For the purpose of illustration, the three critical elements identified are:

1 On-time delivery
2 Order completeness
3 Error- and damage-free delivery.

Each of the three elements needs to be carefully defined and accurately measured. The following definitions are proposed:

1 *On-time delivery* is the number of deliveries in a period that meet the customer's original request divided by the total number of orders received.

$$\frac{\text{Orders delivered on time}}{\text{Total orders received}} \times 100$$

2. *Order completeness* is the percentage of orders shipped complete with the first shipment, and is calculated by dividing the total original order shipped complete by the total orders received.

$$\frac{\text{Orders delivered complete}}{\text{Total orders received}} \times 100$$

3. *Error- and damage-free delivery* can be assessed using invoice adjustments/ credit notes as an indicator of the overall accuracy and quality of the order management and logistics process, and is calculated by dividing the number of 'clean' invoices by the total number of invoices raised.

$$\frac{\text{Clean invoices}}{\text{Total invoices}} \times 100$$

Analysis can be done at the level of the individual customer, by channel, by region, by source of supply (e.g. distribution centre), or at any appropriate level.

Managing the processes that drive the perfect order

How can organisations get anywhere close to achieving the perfect order on every occasion? The answer lies in some of the lessons to be learned from the excellent practitioners of Total Quality Management (TQM). For many years managers of production facilities have recognised that the only way that 100 per cent quality output can be achieved from any process is through the continuous control of that process. In other words, if the process is under control, then the quality of the output can be guaranteed.

Typically, in a production environment managers attempting to improve quality will seek to understand the critical elements of the process where, if a failure were to occur, the quality of the output would be affected. Then, having understood these critical potential 'fail points', the priority is to monitor and control them constantly. More often than not, Statistical Process Control (SPC) methods would be used to assist this task.

These same techniques of process control can be applied successfully to the control of service processes.

The first requirement is that the processes themselves are clearly understood and defined. Typically this involves the detailed mapping and flowcharting of each aspect of the service processes – say, for example, the order management process. It is often the case that once the results of these process mapping exercises are made visible, managers are surprised at the complexity of the processes. Indeed, a benefit of performing this exercise can be that resources are placed behind the re-engineering of those processes to simplify and stream-line them.

The identification of the critical 'fail points' in a service process can be facilitated by the use of cause and effect analysis utilising a fishbone diagram. This simple device is based upon the 80/20 concept, which suggests that 80 per cent of the problems that arise in any process are the result of 20 per cent of the causes. In other words, a few things seem to go wrong more often and cause most of the failures as a result.

Taking as an example an investigation into, say, failure to meet the customers' requested delivery date, we might find a number of more frequently occurring causes – e.g. product not available, carrier performance, lead times too short and so on. If we then seek to investigate the reasons for each of these in turn, reasons for these failures can be identified. By plotting these causes and effects in the form of a fishbone diagram it is possible to begin to identify the key areas where management attention must be focused if failure is to be reduced or eliminated. Figure 2.5 gives an example of a simplified fishbone diagram.

By focusing on the critical areas, ways will often be found to introduce 'fail-safe' systems. In any case it is vital that these critical points be monitored on a continuous basis so that potential problems can quickly be identified. The methods of Statistical Process Control can be used to

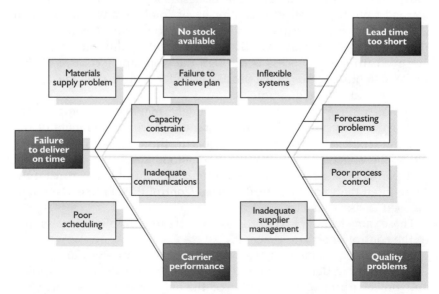

Figure 2.5 An example of cause and effect analysis using a fishbone diagram

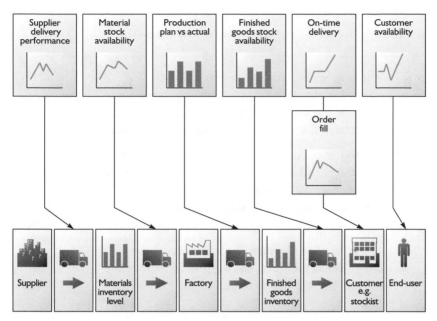

Figure 2.6 Process control and service quality

establish 'control limits' within which these activities must perform. Companies who are serious about perfect order achievement will also have a 'culture of measurement', and will incorporate these measures into their portfolio of key performance indicators.

An example of how one organisation has established a set of key performance indicators from one end of the chain to the other is given in Figure 2.6. Here, the vital determinants of customer service performance are continually monitored and the measures are widely communicated and displayed at all levels in the business.

The underlying theme of this chapter is that enduring customer relationships are based upon the continued delivery of superior service. To achieve the level and quality of service that customers require demands a clear understanding of the critical service issues, market segment by market segment, combined with a commitment to the consistent achievement of the service promise.

Building customer relationships: key issues

■ The importance of customer retention
  ● Retained customers can be more profitable
  ● Calculate the lifetime value of a customer
  ● Understand the reasons for customer defections

■ The emerging concept of relationship marketing
  ● The difference between a transaction and a relationship
  ● Relationships as partnerships
  ● Customer management becomes critical

■ Defining customer service
  ● Look at service through the customers' eyes
  ● Manage service before, during and after the sale
  ● Establish the 'service promise'

■ Developing a market-driven logistics strategy
  ● Research customers' service needs
  ● Define the 'perfect order'
  ● Manage the processes that drive the perfect order

Chapter 3

Creating customer value

The most valuable asset in any business organisation is the strength of its relationships with its customers. Long-term relationships are the basis for enhanced profitability. Such relationships will, however, only exist as long as the customer perceives there to be superior benefit arising from the arrangement. In today's market place the customer has become more demanding as expectations for product performance and service provision continue to increase. The power of the brand or corporate image has diminished as sophisticated customers have come to recognise that there is almost always a choice.

To win and retain customers requires an understanding of what those customers *value* and a focus on the processes whereby that value can consistently be delivered. Clearly there is an equation between the value that customers perceive they are getting and the price they are prepared to pay. Hence the challenge is to identify ways in which customer value can be enhanced through marketing strategies that go beyond the traditional focus on brands and images.

The transition from brand value to customer value

There has been considerable discussion in recent years concerning a purported decline in the strength of brands. Evidence of the growing penetration of private labels and the willingness of customers to select from a portfolio of brands or suppliers adds to the view that the nature of brand loyalty has certainly changed. Whilst there can be no question that strong brands are still a significant asset to a business, whether they are consumer brands or 'corporate brands', it seems that in today's marketing environment there is a need to deliver more than just an image.

Many years ago Theodore Levitt introduced the idea of the 'augmented product', and this concept still holds good today. Essentially, the notion of the augmented product is that it is not sufficient to focus marketing effort on the tangible product features alone. Product features are quickly imitated or cloned by competitors, and in any case, as Levitt would argue, customers don't buy products, they buy benefits. Instead the marketer needs to identify other ways in which value can be delivered to the customer over and above the intrinsic elements embedded in the product itself. RS Components, the parts distributor featured in Chapter 1, has embraced this principle in its marketing efforts.

RS's core offer is the supply of components; time-guaranteed delivery is just one of several value-adding augmentations. It provides product information and advice by telephone or by fax, through its product helplines and via a comprehensive range of web-based services. RS Online allows customers to view and print off 30 000 technical datasheets, provides access to live news feeds from *Electronics Weekly*, and offers on-line technical support by e-mail, together with a range of 'e-tools' such as useful charts, tables and on-line conversions. These services, plus its on-line ordering facility, are presented to the customer in terms of the benefits they offer – accuracy, reliability, convenience, and handling cost reductions.

Figure 3.1 depicts the idea of the augmented product as a 'halo' of benefits and services surrounding the core of functions and features.

This 'halo' obviously includes the intangible aspects of the brand image or 'personality'. However, the argument now is that whilst these brand values will always be important, they are seldom enough. Instead

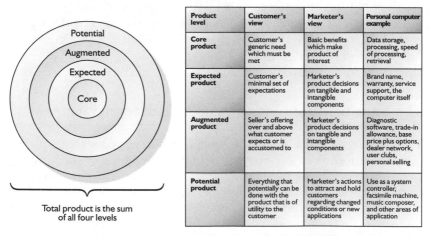

Product level	Customer's view	Marketer's view	Personal computer example
Core product	Customer's generic need which must be met	Basic benefits which make product of interest	Data storage, processing, speed of processing, retrieval
Expected product	Customer's minimal set of expectations	Marketer's product decisions on tangible and intangible components	Brand name, warranty, service support, the computer itself
Augmented product	Seller's offering over and above what customer expects or is accustomed to	Marketer's product decisions on tangible and intangible components	Diagnostic software, trade-in allowance, base price plus options, dealer network, user clubs, personal selling
Potential product	Everything that potentially can be done with the product that is of utility to the customer	Marketer's actions to attract and hold customers regarding changed conditions or new applications	Use as a system controller, facsimile machine, music composer, and other areas of application

Potential / Augmented / Expected / Core

Total product is the sum of all four levels

Figure 3.1 The total product concept (*Source*: Collins, B. (1995) Marketing for engineers. In: *Management for Engineers* (D. Sampson, ed.), p. 415, Longman Cheshire)

they need to be augmented through the wider concept of *customer value*. The customer value concept recognises that market-place success in the new competitive environment will require not only continued investment in the brand, but also *investment in customers*. 'Customer' here means the party or parties who actually buy the product, as distinct from the consumer; the importance of this distinction is that much of marketing investment in the past has been aimed at consumers and not at customers. Owing to the shift in the balance of power in the distribution channels for most products, it is important to recognise that customers (not just consumers) have goals that they seek to achieve, and that the role of the supplier is to help customers achieve those goals.

Defining customer value

What actually is customer value? Put very simply, customer value is created when the perceptions of benefits received from a transaction exceed the total costs of ownership. The same idea can be expressed as a ratio:

$$\text{Customer value} = \frac{\text{Perceptions of benefits}}{\text{Total cost of ownership}}$$

'Total cost of ownership' rather than 'price' is used here because in most transactions there will be costs other than price involved – for example, inventory carrying costs, maintenance costs, running costs, disposal costs etc. In business-to-business markets particularly, as buyers become increasingly sophisticated, the total cost of ownership can be a critical element in the purchase decision. 'Life-cycle costs', as they are referred to in the military and defence industries, have long been a critical issue in procurement decisions in those markets. Figure 3.2 shows the 'iceberg' effect of total costs of ownership, where the immediate purchase price is the only aspect of cost that is visible, whereas below the surface of the water are all the costs that will follow as a result of the purchase decision.

The marketing task is to find ways to enhance customer value by improving the perceived benefits and/or reducing the total costs of ownership. Thus, the goal of marketing and logistics strategy should be to seek to maximise this ratio relative to that of competitors. It could be argued that logistics is almost unique in its ability to impact upon both the numerator and the denominator of this ratio. In the case of business-to-business marketing higher customer value can be delivered through superior logistics performance, enabling our customers to service their customers better but with less inventory and lower ordering costs, for example. The same rationale of enhanced customer value applies to selling to end-users, where perhaps the

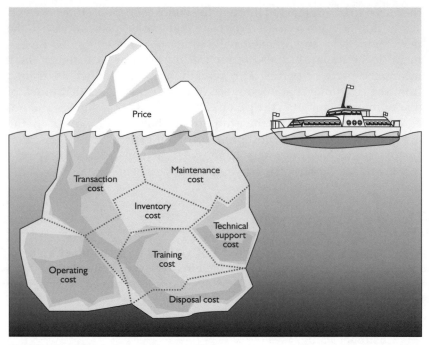

Figure 3.2 The total cost of ownership

benefits might come from, say, increased purchase convenience yet with lowered costs through improved payment terms.

The challenge within the supplying company is to identify unique ways of delivering this enhanced value that competitors will find diffi- cult to imitate, thus providing a basis for sustainable competitive advan- tage. Figure 3.3 highlights some of the ways in which customer value can be enhanced by developing logistics processes that make it easier for customers to service their customers whilst incurring less cost.

It may be necessary to 'educate' customers, who often will not have fully understood the real costs of their existing systems and processes. For example, many organisations still do not recognise the true cost of carrying inventory. Whilst they may place a nominal working capital charge upon departments in relation to the inventory they hold, that charge rarely reflects the actual costs. It has been estimated that it costs an organisation at least 25 per cent per annum of the book value of its inventory to carry it in stock. Inventory here includes raw materials, components, work-in-progress and finished product, as well as goods- in-transit. This figure of 25 per cent includes not only the cost of capital but also the 'opportunity cost' – in other words, the cost of the foregone return that could be made by investing that capital elsewhere. In addition there are the costs of storage and handling, obsolescence, stock losses, insurance and stock management.

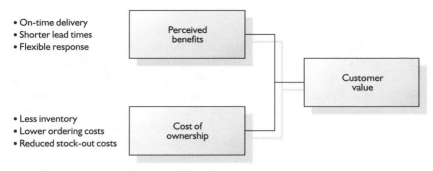

Figure 3.3 Logistics and customer value

Given that a medium to large organisation will have inventory valued in millions of pounds, the annual carrying cost at 25 per cent is considerable. The benefit of any reduction in that inventory is two-fold: first a one-off release of cash, and secondly a continuing reduction in the annual cost of carrying that inventory – which, other things being equal, should go direct to the bottom line.

How inventory carrying costs affect margins

Example:

Direct cost of goods sold	£100
Selling price	£150
Inventory carrying cost	24% p.a.

(i) With one stock turn a year:

Gross margin	£50
Annual inventory carrying cost	£24
∴ Gross margin less inventory cost	£26

(ii) With two stock turns a year:

Gross margin	£50
Annual inventory carrying cost	24/2 = £12
∴ Gross margin less inventory cost	£38

(iii) With four stock turns a year:

Gross margin	£50
Annual inventory carrying cost	24/4 = £6
∴ Gross margin less inventory cost	£44

(iv) With eight stock turns a year:

Gross margin	£50
Annual inventory carrying cost	24/8 = £3
∴ Gross margin less inventory cost	£47

Value-in-use

The whole issue of customer value is inevitably linked to price. Since price forms a part of the total cost of ownership, it follows that there has to be a relationship between the price charged and the customer's perception of value. It also follows that the higher the perception of value, the higher the price that can be charged. Conversely, if price exceeds the perceived value sales will probably decline. It is important to have a clear understanding of the value that customers (and consumers) place on an organisation's offer. This can be termed 'value-in-use', and it should be a priority for all marketing managers to understand better the key elements that comprise it. Figure 3.4 highlights the idea of value-in-use as a balance between perceived benefits (i.e. what the customer 'gets') and the perceived sacrifice (i.e. what the customer 'gives').

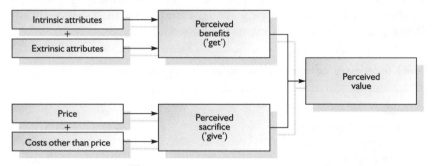

Figure 3.4 The components of value

The perceived benefits derive from the hard, tangible elements of the offer (the intrinsic attributes) and the softer, less tangible elements (the extrinsic attributes). The perceived sacrifice includes all those costs incurred by the customer before, during and after the sale. Again, not all of these costs may be 'hard'; some may be 'soft', such as perceived risk, the costs associated with the time consumed in the purchase process and so on.

Developing a market-driven logistics strategy

The connection between marketing and logistics is not always fully understood within the business. The purpose of the logistics process is to support the marketing strategy of the organisation. Logistics impacts marketing effectiveness through the customer value that is created by superior service.

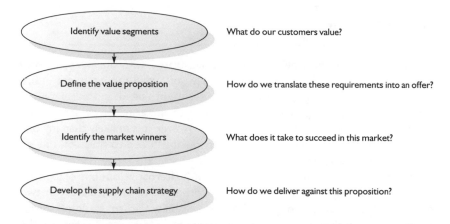

Figure 3.5 Linking customer value to supply chain strategy

Typically organisations have tended to manage those activities they see as 'demand creating' separately from those they consider to be concerned with 'demand satisfaction'. In other words, the classic approach to marketing has focused upon developing and managing the 'offer' and has sought to differentiate that offer through the manipulation of the marketing mix. On the other hand, the mechanisms by which demand is physically satisfied have tended to be seen as a separate responsibility within the business – often termed distribution management. More recently however, companies have come to recognise that in today's markets the processes by which value is delivered to customers need to be managed alongside those by which it is created.

Figure 3.5 suggests a four-stage process to creating a market-driven supply chain strategy, and we will now examine each step in turn.

Identify value segments

It is important to recognise that in any given market there will probably be a number of customer segments that are quite different in their perceptions both of benefits and of sacrifice. In other words, the weights that individual customers or consumers place upon the attributes of the offer will differ, as will their perceptions of actual performance.

As outlined in Chapter 2, it is possible to measure the relative value that customers place upon the different attributes of an offer through the means of 'trade-off analysis'.

Trade-off analysis

The concept of a trade-off can best be illustrated with an example from everyday life. In considering, say, the purchase of a new car, we might desire specific attributes – e.g. performance in terms of speed and acceleration, economy in terms of petrol consumption, size in terms of passenger and luggage capacity, and, of course, low price. However, it is unlikely that any one car will meet all of these requirements, so we are forced to trade-off one or more of these attributes against the others.

The same is true of the customer faced with alternative options of logistics service from a supplier. The buyer might be prepared to sacrifice a day or two on lead time in order to gain delivery reliability, or to trade-off order completeness against improvement in payment terms, etc. Essentially the trade-off technique works by presenting the respondent with feasible combinations of customer service elements and asking for a rank order of preference for those combinations.

Let us take a simple example where a respondent is asked to choose between different levels and combinations of on-time performance, order fill and invoice accuracy. For the sake of example, the following options are presented:

On-time performance	100%
	90%
	80%
Order fill	100%
	90%
	80%
Invoice accuracy	100%
	90%

The various trade-offs can be placed before the respondent as a series of matrices:

		In full	
	100%	90%	80%
On time 100%	1		
90%			
80%			9

	In full		
	100%	90%	80%

Invoice accuracy

	100%	90%	80%
100%	1		
90%			6

	On time		
	100%	90%	80%

Invoice accuracy

	100%	90%	80%
100%	1		
90%			6

The idea is that respondents should complete each matrix to illustrate their preference for service alternatives. Thus, with the first trade-off matrix between on-time delivery and order fill, it is presumed that the most preferred combination would be 100 per cent on time and 100 per cent order fill. But what about the other combinations? Here respondents are asked to complete each matrix to identify their preferences. An example of a typical response is given below.

	In full		
	100%	90%	80%

On time

	100%	90%	80%
100%	1	2	4
90%	3	5	7
80%	6	8	9

	In full		
	100%	90%	80%

Invoice accuracy

	100%	90%	80%
100%	1	3	5
90%	2	4	6

| | On time | | |
	100%	90%	80%
Invoice accuracy 100%	1	2	4
90%	3	4	6

Using computer analysis, the implicit 'importance weights' that underlie the initial preference rankings can be generated. For the data in the example above, the following weights emerge:

Service element		Importance weight
On-time performance:	100%	+0.480
	90%	0
	80%	−0.480
Order fill:	100%	+0.456
	90%	0
	80%	−0.456
Invoice accuracy:	100%	+0.239
	90%	−0.239

For this respondent, on-time performance would seem to be marginally more important than order fill, and both were in the region of twice as important as invoice accuracy.

Having determined the importance attached by different respondents to each of the service attributes, the next step is to see if any similarities of preference amongst respondents emerge as this can provide the basis for a powerful means of market segmentation.

Once the different 'value segments' that exist within a market can be identified, then we can begin to develop marketing and logistics strategies specifically for those segments. Figure 3.6 offers a generic example of such a segmentation exercise in the car market.

This technique of mapping customer perceptions of benefit against their appraisal of total cost of ownership can provide a powerful basis for competitive analysis. Figure 3.7 suggests that if both perceived benefits and total cost of ownership are measured relative to competition, then an acceptable position for an organisation would be in the diagonal of the box. The lower right-hand corner would reflect a perception of inferior value, and likewise the top left-hand corner a perception of superior value. Organisations finding themselves in this

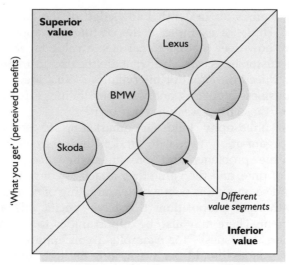

Figure 3.6 Value segmentation

top left-hand corner might want to ensure that they are not 'giving the shop away' – in other words, does their position of perceived superior value enable them to make an upward price correction?

By focusing on those things the customer attaches most value to, the supplying organisation is more likely to win and retain business.

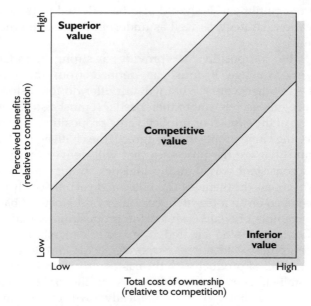

Figure 3.7 Relative customer value

Doing this requires an in-depth knowledge of the customers' own value chain. Thus, for example, if the customer is another business organisation, how does that customer create value for *its* customers? What are its customers' costs, and what are the opportunities for those costs to be reduced through our intervention? What are the characteristics of its business processes, and what possibilities exist for a greater integration of those processes with our own?

The same philosophy holds for marketing to end-users. The supplying organisation needs to understand the lifestyle of the consumers, the problems and pressures they face, the relative importance of time, and the value they attach to convenience, ease of operation and so on. In this way a better targeting of customers can be achieved with value propositions that have specific relevance to the chosen segment. There may also be opportunities to emphasise total cost of ownership issues – for example, a concentrated washing-up liquid that needs less liquid per wash, long-life light bulbs that need changing less often, paints that need no undercoats, and oils that run cooler so fewer engine oil changes are needed.

Define the value proposition

The value proposition is quite simply a statement of how, where and when value is to be created for specific customers or market segments. The value proposition should form the guiding principles around which all the activities of the firm are based, from product development to order fulfilment. It should also be reflected in the marketing communications strategy, as well as underpinning the internal values of the business.

For a value proposition to provide a strong foundation for competitive advantage it must be defined from the customer's viewpoint – in other words: what will our offer do for customers that they will recognise as relevant to their needs? It must also be set against the backdrop of the explicit or implicit value propositions of competing offers. Once the value proposition is agreed, the challenge to logistics is to create and manage the processes that will deliver that value in a timely and consistent way. Linking logistics strategy and marketing strategy is of course the theme of this book, and yet only rarely do we see the two managed on an integrated, customer value-focused basis.

A good example of a successful value proposition is that provided by Dell Computer, who created a market leadership position in personal computers sold to the corporate sector. In effect what Dell offer is a customised product with the customer's proprietary software already installed, delivered within days of the order. Dell is not offering superior technology or dramatically lower prices, but rather a highly responsive and bespoke service.

Avon calling

In the age of infinite consumer choice, where immediate availability is taken as a prerequisite for success in FMCG marketing, the very notion of a business that relies overwhelmingly on door-to-door sales and a two- to three-week fulfilment cycle sounds like a legacy from The Land that Time Forgot. Nevertheless, it is a formula that continues to work well for Avon, the world's largest manufacturer of cosmetics, fragrances and toiletries.

Avon's core offer consists of competitively priced, quality beauty products (mostly internally sourced) and gifts. In recent years the company has started selling its wares over the Internet, but the bulk of its business worldwide continues to be conducted through its traditional distribution channel – a network of 3 million independent sales representatives. The network spans 140 countries over six continents. The vast majority of the representatives are women, and all are rewarded on a commission-only basis. Between them these 'Avon ladies' execute over a billion transactions per year with a total value of over US$5 billion, making Avon one of the world's largest direct selling companies.

As an organisation, Avon is acutely aware of the importance of the personal relationships between its customers (the representatives) and the ultimate consumers. It knows that this social interaction is an important element in its value proposition, because it makes buying and selling beauty products fun. In the words of one senior manager:

> We have a very loyal customer base and the kind of turnover we do is an indication that people like the way we do business. They like the social aspect of door-to-door, they like dealing with family, with friends and in the workplace.

In the UK, Avon launches a new sales campaign roughly every three weeks. Representatives receive the new brochures, distribute them to their customers, and collect and place orders. It is up to Avon to ensure that those orders are met.

> A consumer will have waited two to three weeks for her product and she will expect her representative to arrive with that product as promised. Loyal customers who have been with us for years and understand how we do business would forgive us if just for once we could not supply an item. But it's different with a new customer, the first time we failed to deliver a product we would lose her. Not only would we lose the customer and maybe her associates, we could lose the representative too. If we don't deliver the product, she is the one who has to deal with the 'moment of truth', she loses her earning opportunity and she has the embarrassment of letting her customer down. That means that delivering a perfect order to the representative is absolutely essential.

Avon acknowledges the importance of protecting those all-important value-adding customer relationships by making the 'perfect order' a key performance indicator. Internally it also promotes customer service principles not only as a way of drawing its marketing and logistics functions together but also as a way of focusing all minds within the organisation on the role they play in ensuring that the 'Avon ladies' keep on calling.

Identify the market winners

As previously suggested, in any purchase situation there will only be three or four key determinants driving the choice of supplier or product. These key drivers are what might be termed the key success factors or 'market winners'. Sometimes it will be product performance or price that determines the decision, but in other situations availability, responsiveness and reliability may be the market winners. Understanding the nature of these key success factors is a vital prerequisite for successful supply chain design. In the case of Dell, the market winners are clearly responsiveness and customised solutions. US-based Wal-Mart, the world's biggest retailer, has long seen low prices as the key to their success. At Zara, the Spanish-based high street fashion retailer, the ability to respond quickly to market trends has been a key determinant.

Understanding the market winners is a virtual precursor to the design of supply chain strategies. The strategy adopted must then be consistent with the achievement of those market-winning goals, but all too often this is not the case. Furthermore, it should also be recognised that preferences may vary between local/regional/national markets or between market segments. As a result, an organisation may have to devise a series of supply chain strategies to meet the requirements of differing market-winning criteria. Many fast-moving consumer goods companies, for example, have differentiated their supply chains according to whether they are servicing 'everyday low-price' retailers or, alternatively, retail customers with frequent promotions demanding a more agile response.

Develop the supply chain strategy

If the preceding three steps have been followed, the choice of supply chain strategy will usually be fairly apparent. Using the examples of Dell, Wal-Mart and Zara, it is interesting to see how their supply chain thinking has been clearly linked to their marketing strategy. Dell has close links with a small number of strategic suppliers who physically co-locate alongside Dell's assembly operations. Finished inventory is minimal and products are assembled to order, utilising advanced planning systems and shared information along the supply chain. Wal-Mart, on the other hand, has consistently focused on developing the most cost-efficient inbound logistics process in its sector. It was an early innovator in sharing data captured at the point of sale with suppliers, enabling suppliers to manage inventory far more effectively.

The focus of Zara's supply chain is on agility. Operating in a volatile fashion market, Zara captures information on trends in its target markets and, utilising a network of small suppliers, can respond within days. Because they produce in small batches, they can minimise the risk inherent in long supply chains – that is, they can respond rapidly to both upswings and downswings in demand.

Value delivery systems

The means by which value is 'delivered' to customers is clearly critical to maintaining competitive advantage. When we talk of delivery systems we refer not only to the physical delivery of products or the presentation of service, but also to the marketing channels employed, the flexibility of response, the linking of buyer–supplier logistics and information systems, and so on. In other words, the design of the value delivery system should be seen as a powerful means of engineering stronger linkages between the customer's and the supplier's value chains. One company that has taken the customer (and consumer) value issue seriously is Procter & Gamble (P&G), which has redirected its entire business focus towards competing through enhanced customer value. One way in which this has manifested itself in North America is through its strategy of 'value pricing'. In an attempt to reduce the prices of its products to consumers, thus enhancing the value, P&G sought to remove significant cost from the supply chain – having estimated that logistics costs in the USA came to $1 billion a year on sales of $15 billion.

Much of this cost was generated as the result of promotional activity, from promotions aimed both at the trade and at end-users. For example, wherever promotional price cuts on wholesale prices were made (which was frequently), retailers would take advantage of these markdowns by 'forward buying' – in other words, they would buy more than they required for immediate sales requirements and then sell the remaining goods at full price later. This would lead to big surges in demand in one period, followed by a downturn in demand in the next. As a result, some P&G factories were only running at 35–65 per cent of their rated efficiency. On top of this, the company estimated that it was making 55 daily price changes on some 80 brands, leading to order inaccuracy and invoice errors. The real costs of these promotions were significant, and far outweighed any tactical sales advantage.

The idea behind value pricing is to offer a guaranteed low price to the trade for a finite contractual period. This price is lower than the previous list price, but will not fluctuate during the contract period and neither will there be tactical price promotions. As a result both parties should benefit – as well as the final consumer.

Impacting the customers' profitability

In business-to-business marketing, a clear measure of customer value is the impact that the supplier has upon its customers' profitability. In other words, if by our actions we can either increase the customers' chance of selling more product and/or reduce their costs of ownership, then customer value has been created.

A good example of this is provided in marketing to the retail trade, where 'return on shelf space' is often seen as a critical issue by the retailer. Return on shelf space can be expressed as:

$$\frac{\text{Profit}}{\text{Shelf space}}$$

which can be further expressed as:

$$\frac{\text{Profit}}{\text{Sales}} \times \frac{\text{Sales}}{\text{Shelf space}}$$

This is an important relationship, since the first ratio (profit/sales) is more commonly referred to as 'the margin' and it is here that conventional buyer–supplier negotiations have focused.

However, by improving the second ratio (sales/shelf space), which might be termed shelf-space productivity, then even a low margin can be leveraged into higher profitability. For example, many continental European discount retailers have net margins of 2 per cent or less, yet with high levels of sales per unit of shelf space they can achieve a significant leverage as far as overall return on investment is concerned.

Thus a supplier's strategy that focuses upon improving the retailer's sales per square metre or per linear metre might win more of that shelf space for the supplier's own products. There are a number of ways in which such an improvement can be achieved – for example, by redesigning the pack so that it has a better 'footprint' on the shelf and occupies less space, and at the same time developing a 'quick response' replenishment system so that the inventory velocity on the shelf is increased, the supplier can significantly impact shelf-space profitability.

More and more retailers are now starting to measure the profitability of their shelf space, particularly as they move towards a strategy in which products are grouped into categories and those categories are then managed against profit goals. This idea of category management will be explored further in Chapter 6.

One tool that is widely used to assess shelf-space profitability is a measurement known as 'Direct Product Profit' (DPP). To a retailer, direct product profit is a measure of an item's actual contribution to overall profit. It goes beyond the traditional measure of gross margin by:

- Adjusting the gross margin for each item to reflect deals, allowances, net forward buy income, prompt payment, discounts, etc.
- Identifying and measuring the costs that can be directly attributed to individual products (direct product costs like labour, space, inventory and transport).

Direct product profit

This is the net profit contribution from the sale of a product after allowances are added and all costs that can be rationally allocated or assigned to an individual product are subtracted.

	Sales
−	Cost of goods sold
=	Gross margin
+	Allowances and discounts
=	Adjusted gross margin
−	Warehouse costs
	● Labour (labour model − case, cube, weight)
	● Occupancy (space and cube)
	● Inventory (average inventory)
−	Transportation costs (cube)
−	Retails costs
	● Stocking labour
	● Front-end labour
	● Occupancy
	● Inventory
=	Direct product profit

Since product characteristics and associated costs vary so much item by item (e.g. cube, weight, case pack count, handling costs, space occupied, turnover), the retailer needs to calculate the DPP at the item level. Similarly, because shelf space is the limiting factor for the retailer the key measure of performance becomes DPP/square metre or even DPP/cubic metre.

The key issue to the retailer is 'shelf yield', which is calculated as follows:

$$\frac{\text{DPP per item} \times \text{sales per week}}{\text{Square metres occupied}}$$

An item could have a low gross margin but low direct product costs, high sales and low space occupancy, so delivering a high shelf yield. Conversely, a high gross margin product with high direct product costs and low sales per week occupying more shelf space will deliver a low shelf yield.

Consequently the challenge to the supplier is to seek to develop products (including, crucially, the pack design) and logistics processes that deliver better shelf yield for the retailer. Companies like Procter & Gamble have consciously built issues like these into all their product and logistics strategies, even to the extent of redesigning the packaging to improve shelf-space occupancy.

By understanding in detail the customers' business, cost structures and the dynamics of their markets, the supplier can begin to tailor its marketing logistics strategy so that significant improvements in customer value can be achieved. As the benefit to the customer becomes evident, so too should the return to the supplier in the form of extra business.

Whilst return on shelf space and DPP are issues specific to the retail sector, the general principle of focusing upon ways of positively impacting the customers' profit-and-loss account and balance sheet is pivotal to the creation of customer value in any industry.

Understanding the costs-to-serve

Not all customers are equally profitable, and a goal of effective logistics management should be to focus the resources of the business upon those customers where either current or potential profitability is highest.

Underlying this idea is the well-known 80/20 principle, or the Pareto Rule. The 80/20 principle tells us that not only is 80 per cent of the total sales volume of a business generated by just 20 per cent of the customers, but also that the likelihood is that 80 per cent of the total costs of servicing all the customers will be caused by only 20 per cent of customers (but probably not the same 20 per cent). Whilst the proportion may not be exactly 80/20, it will generally be in this region.

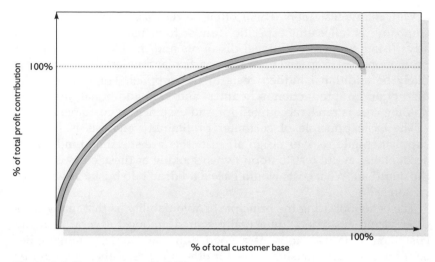

Figure 3.8 Customer profitability

Figure 3.8 illustrates the shape of the distribution of profits that results from the uneven spread of revenues and costs across the customer base.

From this example it can be seen that there is a 'tail' of customers who are actually unprofitable and who therefore reduce total profit contribution!

The challenge to customer management, therefore, is first to identify the real profitability of customers, and secondly to develop logistics strategies that will improve the profitability of all customers.

Why should customers differ in their real profitability? The first reason is that different customers will often buy a different mix of products. Individual products have different gross margins, so clearly the mix of products purchased will impact upon the profitability of specific customers.

Beyond this, however, it must be recognised that there are also substantial differences in the costs of servicing individual customers. It has been said that profitability is largely determined by what happens *after* the point of production.

The costs of service begin with the order itself – how long does the sales person spend with the customer? Is there a key account manager whose time is spent wholly or in part working with that customer? What commissions do we pay on sales?

Then there are the order processing costs, which themselves will differ according to the number of lines on the order, the number of orders and their complexity. Beyond this there will be transport costs, materials handling costs and often inventory and warehousing costs – particularly if the products are held on a dedicated basis for customers, as with own-label products.

With many customers it will often be the case that the supplying company is allocating specific funds for customer promotions, advertising support, additional discounts and the like. In the case of promotions (e.g. a special pack for a particular retailer) there will most likely be additional hidden costs to the supplier. For example, the disruption to production schedules and the additional inventory holding cost is rarely accounted for and assigned to customers.

The basic principle of customer profitability analysis is that the supplier should seek to assign all costs that are specific to individual accounts. A useful test to apply when looking at these costs is to ask the question: 'What costs would I *avoid* if I didn't do business with this customer?'

The benefit of using the principle of 'avoidability' is that many costs of servicing customers are actually shared amongst several or many customers. The warehouse is a good example – unless the supplier could release warehousing space for other purposes, then it would be incorrect to allocate a proportion of the total warehousing costs to a particular customer. A checklist of costs to include when drawing up the profit-and-loss account for specific customers is provided here.

The customer profit-and-loss account

Revenues

Less

Costs (attributable costs only)

- Net sales value

- Cost of sales (actual product mix)
- Commissions
- Sales calls
- Key account management time
- Trade bonuses and special discount
- Order processing costs
- Promotional costs (visible and hidden)
- Merchandising costs
- Non-standard packaging/unitisation
- Dedicated inventory holding costs
- Dedicated warehouse space
- Materials handling costs
- Transport costs
- Documentation/communications costs
- Returns/refusals
- Trade credit (actual payment period)

Whilst it may not be practicable to undertake such analysis for individual accounts, it should be possible to select representative

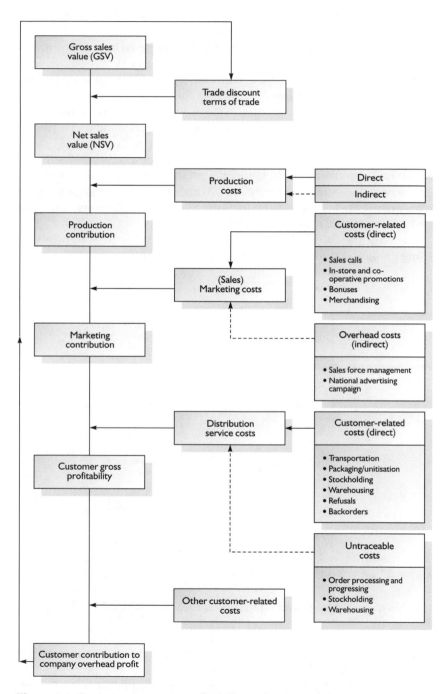

Figure 3.9 Customer account profitability: a basic model

customers on a sample basis so that a view can be gained of the relative costs associated with different types of accounts or distribution channels – or even market segments.

The recommended procedure for implementing customer profitability analysis is highlighted in Figure 3.9 (see page 61).

What often emerges from these studies is that the largest customers in terms of volume (or even revenue) may not be the most profitable because of their high costs of service – for example, they may gain bigger volume-based discounts, require more frequent deliveries to more dispersed locations, or insist on non-standard pallets.

What, ultimately, should be the purpose of this analysis? Ideally we require all our customers to be profitable in the medium to long term, and where customers currently are profitable we should seek to build and extend that profitability further. The British Airways example given later in this chapter illustrates the principle.

The customer profitability matrix illustrated in Figure 3.10 provides some generalised guidance for strategic direction.

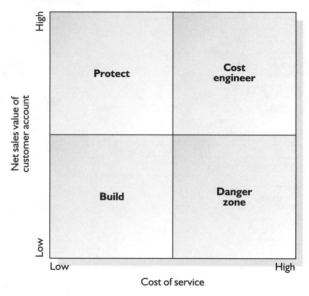

Figure 3.10 Customer profitability matrix

Briefly, the appropriate strategies for each quadrant of the matrix are:

Build – These customers are relatively cheap to service, but their net sales value is low. Can volume be increased without a proportionate increase in the costs of service? Can our sales team be directed to seek to influence these customers' purchases towards a more profitable sales mix?

Danger zone – These customers should be looked at very carefully. Is there any medium- to long-term prospect either of improving net sales value or reducing the costs of service? Is there a strategic reason for keeping them? Do we need them for their volume even if their profit contribution is low?

Cost engineer – These customers could be more profitable if the costs of servicing them could be reduced. Is there any scope for increasing drop sizes? Could deliveries be consolidated? If new accounts in the same geographic area were developed, would it make delivery more economic? Is there a cheaper way of gathering orders from these customers, e.g. telesales?

Protect – The high net sales value customers who are relatively cheap to service are worth their weight in gold. The strategy for these customers should be to seek relationships that make the customer less likely to want to seek alternative suppliers. At the same time we should constantly seek opportunities to develop the volume of business that we do with these customers whilst keeping strict control of costs.

British Airways – understanding customer profitability

For many years British Airways (BA) maintained its seemingly unassailable position as the UK national carrier. Things began to change in the 1990s, when deregulation of the European airline industry opened the way for new budget airlines to undercut BA on short-haul flights.

In 1996, BA reported losses for the first time in years. The company's management moved quickly to introduce what turned out to be a misguided recovery plan. The first strand of the strategy involved aggressive measures to build market share by targeting European transfer passengers transiting through BA's second hub at Gatwick Airport. The second strand involved an equally aggressive programme of cost cutting. The cost cuts were deeply unpopular with BA staff, who responded with industrial action.

The following year BA announced its intention to launch 'Go', a no-frills airline of its own, based at Stansted Airport. Go enabled BA to compete directly on the short-haul routes with fast-growing budget operators such as easyJet and Ryanair, without compromising the integrity of the full-service core brand.

For the core BA brand, deregulation was seen as an opportunity to extend the airline's global reach. Its aspirations were reflected by a decision to cast off its 'Anglo-centric' Union Jack tail fins, spending £60m on a series of new ethnic designs – 'an acknowledgement that 60% of BA's passengers now hailed from outside the UK'. The move was later deemed to have been one of the most outstanding corporate PR disasters of the decade. What BA had not anticipated was that the new tail fin designs would alienate the British-based business passengers.

The business travellers were already irritated by the effect of the steep increase in the volume of travellers pouring through BA's overcrowded Heathrow and Gatwick hubs and by the simultaneous drop in service caused by industrial action and plummeting staff morale. The company would later come to realise that although these passengers represented a relatively small proportion of BA's total volume, they accounted for most of its profits. In the meantime, things went from bad to worse for the self-proclaimed 'World's Favourite Airline'.

By 1999, the collapse of many Asian currencies precipitated a knock-on collapse in demand for air travel around the region, leading in turn to overcapacity and falling fares. The Asian downturn prompted many airlines to switch capacity to transatlantic routes, forcing down prices there too. Transatlantic services had historically yielded about 80 per cent of BA's profits.

By now, though, BA had recognised that its cost structure and full-service position would not permit it to compete head-on with the budget carriers. The company still sought to protect its shrinking margins, with further cost-cutting measures relating to finance, staffing and catering. Controversially, BA also decided to cut capacity by 12 per cent over a three-year period. The cuts accompanied a switch in strategic focus, which would see BA pouring considerable effort into targeting and retaining the high-margin business passengers:

> What we are talking about is really changing the mix of our business from about a level of 14–15% of business to about 16–17%. It is that kind of level. It is not an enormous change. Most of our passengers are still going to be economy class and we welcome them. We never forget that today's back-packer is tomorrow's business traveller ... An additional 1 or 2% shift in passenger traffic makes a huge difference. It makes the entire business more profitable and repays our investment in products and services.
>
> (Simon Walker, BA Director of Communications,
> BBC World Service, 13 November 1999)

To woo the premium price passengers, BA decided to invest in a newer but smaller fleet of aircraft, plus £600m ($970m) worth of new service products to be introduced between January 2000 and the end of 2002. The investment was to be the biggest of its kind in airline history. The innovations were the result of extensive market research; they were designed to appeal to upmarket travellers by setting new industry benchmarks for comfort, design and convenience. In business class these innovations included a 'lounge in the sky', featuring the world's first fully flat bed for travellers who need to work and sleep in private on long-haul trips. First class cabins were to be revamped too, and a totally refurbished Concorde would be taking to the skies. Back on terra firma the company proudly announced upgrades to airport terminals, check-ins and lounges, including a completely new terminal at New York JFK.

At the higher-volume, lower-margin end of the business, BA was still determined to maintain a price premium by differentiating its offer from that of its no-frills competitors. Long-haul economy passenger were also offered a better standard of travel with the new World Traveller Plus class cabins, with more space and facilities than other economy products, as well as a doubled hand-baggage allowance. On the short-haul routes the company rolled out its new Club Europe; here, though, BA was looking to reduce its order handling costs by cutting its commissions to travel agents.

The strategy appeared to be working. In May 2001 BA revealed a massive jump in profits over the previous year, up from £5 million to £150 million. Capacity was cut by 3.3 per cent and manpower by 4.3 per cent, while passenger yields were up 7.7 per cent – the biggest year-on-year rise since privatisation in 1987. The airline made it clear that it intended to reduce capacity by another 8–9 per cent in 2001, with further reductions in 2002. The capacity cuts saw a related reduction in the cost base, particularly at London Gatwick airport, where BA was reorganising its loss-making short-haul operations. The European network had made operating losses of £811 million in the five years to March 2001. Far from improving profitability, raising volumes of traffic on the short-haul network had simply increased BA's losses. In recognition of this, several unprofitable routes had been axed, more were to go, and the fleet was to be reshuffled to improve capacity utilisation.

In June 2001 the company confirmed its intention to withdraw completely from the short-haul budget market with the sale of 'Go'. The stand-alone subsidiary was said to be cannibalising some of BA's core business, turning high-margin passengers into low-margin ones.

Ideally organisations should seek to develop an accounting system that would routinely collect and analyse the data on customer profitability. Unfortunately most accounting systems are product-focused rather than customer-focused. Likewise, cost reporting is traditionally on a functional rather than a transactional basis. Hence we know, for example, the costs of the transport function as a whole or the costs of making a particular product, but what we do not know are the costs of delivering a specific mix of product to a particular customer.

The challenge to any business is to define more clearly the value that it seeks to provide for its chosen customer segments, and then to focus on the means whereby that value can be delivered most cost-effectively. Customer value has become the major differentiator in many markets, and the contribution that logistics can make to enhancing that differentiation is now more widely recognised within leading companies.

Creating customer value: key issues

- The change in emphasis from brand value to customer value
  - Customer value is the difference between perceived benefits and total cost of ownership
  - Focus on the value proposition
  - Understand the 'market winners'

- Can we impact customers' costs of ownership?
  - Reduce their costs of stockholding
  - Reduce their stock-out costs
  - Improve their 'direct product profit'

- Customer profitability management
  - Not all customers are equally profitable
  - Understand the costs-to-serve
  - Differentiate service strategy according to customer priority

Chapter 4

Time-based competition

In recent years, one of the most significant developments in the way that companies manage their operations and formulate their competitive strategies has been the focus on *time*. There are clearly many ways in which firms compete and through which they seek to gain advantage over their rivals. However, the ability to move quickly, whether in new product development or in replenishing customers' inventories, is increasingly recognised as a prerequisite for market-place success.

The late twentieth century saw the emergence of the *time-sensitive* customer. These time-sensitive customers can be found in every type of market, whether high-tech markets where short life cycles demand short lead times, consumer durable manufacturing where just-in-time assembly requires just-in-time deliveries, or everyday living where the pressures of managing a more complex, hectic lifestyle have led us to seek convenience in, for example, banking, shopping and eating.

Whole industries have grown up around time compression, from overnight delivery to fast food. Technology has facilitated this process – cellular telephones, fax and satellite communications have all contributed to the continued search for the achievement of quicker response to the demands that customers place upon companies. Now, quality is measured not just in terms of product performance but also on delivery performance. Few industries have been immune from these pressures, and managers must constantly seek ever-more innovative ways to squeeze time out of every business process. Indeed, the main driver behind the Business Process Re-engineering (BPR) philosophy has been the search for more time-effective ways of doing things.

Time reduction does not only lead to faster response to customer needs but, just as importantly, can also lead to cost reduction and greater flexibility. Drawing an analogy with an oil pipeline, the longer the pipeline from, say, a refinery to a distant market place, the slower it will be to respond to a change in demand in that market place. At the same time, the longer the pipeline, the more oil is contained within it – hence the greater the working capital that is locked up. 'Time is money' may be a cliché, but in today's competitive market place it has never been truer.

Lack of responsiveness in logistics processes can heighten the risks of both stock-outs (and thus lost sales) and over-stocked situations (leading to markdowns or stock write-offs).

Supply chain disruptions impact shareholder returns

Research in the USA (Singhal, V. and Hendricks, K. (2002) How supply chain glitches torpedo shareholder value, *Supply Chain Management Review*, Jan./Feb., 18–24) has highlighted a direct connection between problems in the supply chain and the share price of the business. On average bad news from the supply chain will reduce share prices by 7.5 per cent, but this will often trigger a longer-term decline averaging an 18.5 per cent reduction in shareholder return. The most common causes for these supply chain disruptions are shown in Figure 4.1, along with the consequent immediate impact on shareholder return.

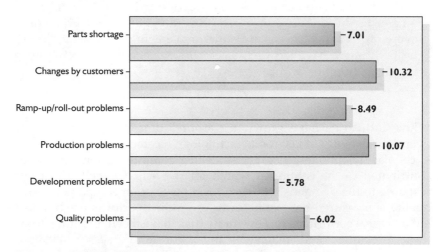

Figure 4.1 Reasons for supply chain disruption and their impact on shareholder returns (*Source*: Singhal, V. and Hendricks, K. (2002) How supply chain glitches torpedo shareholder value, *Supply Chain Management Review*, Jan./Feb., 18–24)

In 2001 the networking giant Cisco found itself with a $2.25bn inventory write-off, following a sudden downturn in demand for equipment. Over the previous five years the company had grown accustomed to exponentially increasing demand for network equipment. To keep pace it had taken to placing big orders for communications chips, optical lasers and sub-assembly boards from its suppliers. However, sales had slumped with the dot.com collapse, leaving Cisco with warehouses overflowing with billions of dollars worth of excess inventory. The market value of the stock had subsequently dropped below the original cost of acquisition, resulting in an inventory charge for that quarter. Most of the inventory had to be scrapped or destroyed. It could not be sold because it had been specially produced to Cisco's requirements.

The cash-to-cash cycle

In any business, a critical measure of performance is the 'cash-to-cash' cycle. Put very simply, this is a measure of the total cash that is locked up in the 'pipeline' from when materials or components are purchased from suppliers to when the finished product is sold and the cash is received from customers.

One of the surprising features of the cash-to-cash cycle is just how long that cycle can be for many companies. It is not unusual to find pipelines within a business that are six months or more in length. Even more surprising is the fact that so many companies fail to measure (and hence to manage) these pipelines.

'End-to-end' pipeline time reflects all the stages of the logistics process, including: procurement lead times; in-bound transit time; time spent in manufacturing, assembly and internal operations; order processing times; delivery times; and, of course, time spent when nothing is happening and materials, work-in-progress and finished goods are 'sitting still' as inventory. Figure 4.2 highlights the ways in which time in the pipeline builds up.

It must be remembered that every day spent in the pipeline represents a cost to the business. Quite apart from the cost of funding the working capital employed there is the 'opportunity cost' – in other words, whilst cash is locked up in the pipeline it cannot be put to use elsewhere in the business or, indeed, invested elsewhere. In large organisations where a day's sales can be measured in millions of pounds or dollars, then the cost of even an extra day of pipeline time will be considerable.

For example, when employees of a large aerospace company calculated the inventory holding costs of incoming radar systems, they found that the potential savings were huge. To put the scale of the costs into perspective, they calculated that, were it possible to have such

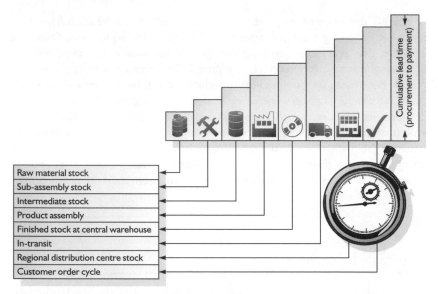

Figure 4.2 How long is the logistics pipeline?

complex and expensive pieces of equipment delivered on a just-in-time basis, the company could afford to have each system delivered in a brand new BMW car, write-off the car, and still be saving money!

Taking time out of the pipeline will bring with it many benefits, including:

- A one-off release of capital
- A continuing benefit through the reduced cost of financing a shorter pipeline
- Shorter response times, and hence higher service levels
- Less vulnerability to market-place volatility
- More flexibility in meeting precise customer requirements (e.g. options, pack sizes, colours, etc.).

Figure 4.3 demonstrates, at a generalised level, the effect that reducing pipeline time can have on profitability. The upward sloping line shows the cumulative build-up of cost from one end of the pipeline to the other. If time in the pipeline can be compressed, then it is likely that both the fixed and variable costs can be reduced as the cost profile is 'shrunk'. The final result is greater profit per unit, with the possibility, in a time-sensitive market, of greater sales.

There are three dimensions to time-based competition that must be managed in a coherent and integrated way if the organisation is to become more agile and responsive – and more profitable:

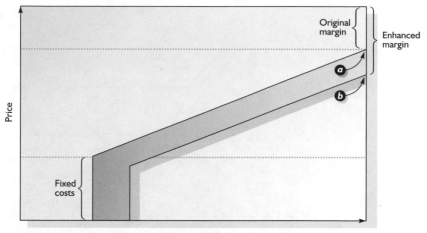

(a) Cumulative costs before pipeline reduction
(b) Cumulative costs after pipeline reduction

Figure 4.3 The impact of pipeline time on profit

1 *Time to market* – how long does it take the business to recognise a market opportunity, translate this into a product or service and to bring it to the market?
2 *Time to serve* – how long does it take to capture a customer's order and to deliver or install the product to the customer's satisfaction?
3 *Time to react* – how long does it take to adjust the output of the business in response to volatile demand? Can the 'tap' be turned on or off quickly?

Time to market

Innovation and timely new product development is a vital source of competitive advantage in any market. This has always been the case, but it is made all the more necessary as a result of shortening product life cycles. The product life cycle represents the growth and decline in demand for a specific product in a particular market. Whilst it is rare for these life cycles to be smooth and predictable, one feature seems to be common across most industries and technologies, and that is that these life cycles are getting shorter.

In some cases changing technology radically shortens the saleable life of a product. The personal computer market provides a classic example of this, to the extent that life cycles for some products are twelve months or less. In other cases changes in consumer taste, fashion or competitive pressures lead to rapid obsolescence or a switch in consumer preference.

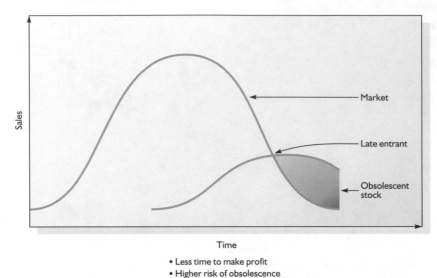

Figure 4.4 Shorter life cycles make timing crucial

These shortening life cycles make timing critical. Figure 4.4 highlights the double jeopardy facing companies that are slow to respond to market-place changes. In the first instance, a late entrant will miss a sales opportunity that may well be captured by competitors. In the second case the company might find that just as its shipments into the market are getting up to speed, demand is already falling away – perhaps in response to the arrival of the next technology or competitive offer. The likely result is that the company will be left with obsolete or outdated inventory, resulting in markdowns or even write-offs.

One of the keys to speeding up time to market is the ability to be as close to the customer as possible. Continuous customer contact as a source of innovation is not a new idea, but is not always practised. Whilst many companies indulge in *ad hoc* market research, few companies recognise the need to monitor customer and market trends on an ongoing basis. 'Market understanding' is a prerequisite for innovation – if we are slow to read the market, it doesn't matter how quick we are in product design and manufacturing.

This type of continuous market research also implies a willingness to gauge customer reactions from the moment the product hits the market, and to be prepared to modify the product as many times as may be necessary. Japanese consumer electronic companies such as Sony tend to be particularly good at making changes on the run. It has been suggested that rather than using the traditional Western approach to product design and development, which might be thought of as 'ready, aim, fire', the Japanese instead go for a concept of 'ready, fire, aim'! What this means is that because Japanese companies have focused on flexibility and speed, they are able to launch products almost at prototype stage and then quickly modify them in the light of customer response.

However, it takes more than a close contact with customers to reduce the time taken from the drawing board to the market. It used to take from ten to fifteen years in the automobile industry to take an idea from concept to the dealer's showroom. Now companies like Ford can introduce new models in less than two years. The secret is 'simultaneous' or 'parallel' engineering. Traditional product development was a sequential process characterised by a series of quite separate stages, such as R&D, engineering, prototyping, marketing research and so on. Often ideas would get some way down the chain before it was realised that the concept needed revision in some way, and hence 'back to the drawing board' was a frequently encountered cry.

Now the best companies create self-managed, multidisciplinary teams that are given the authority to take whatever actions are necessary to bring the product to market. So, for example, innovative companies like 3M will bring research scientists, production specialists, market researchers and logistics managers together and encourage them to work as a team to solve problems and to work in 'parallel'. Not only is time significantly compressed through this approach, but problems are also more readily identified and solved.

Bringing logistics management into the new product development process can prove beneficial. For example, if product design decisions can take account of transport and storage requirements, then significant improvements to lifetime profits might result. Again, having logistics management involved early in the design process may well lead to the identification of potential problems if components or packaging materials with long replenishment lead times are being considered. Often product modifications made at the design stage can have significant effects on total pipeline time once the product is commercialised, because materials and components with long replenishment lead times are avoided.

Time to serve

'Time to serve' can be defined as the elapsed time from the initiation of an order by a customer to the final delivery or installation. Inevitably in a time-sensitive world, shorter order cycles can provide significant competitive advantage. Closely coupled with the demands from customers for shorter delivery lead times is the requirement for *reliability*. In an environment where more organisations are seeking to minimise their inventories and manage on a 'just-in-time' basis, suppliers must be able to guarantee delivery times – even down to time windows as narrow as an hour.

Managing the order-to-delivery cycle requires an understanding of the order fulfilment process and the causes of time consumption and variability within it. The goal should be to seek to simplify and streamline what can often be an unnecessarily complex sequence of activities, performed usually one after the other in a linear manner. Re-engineering the order fulfilment process to reduce time consumption and variability involves a fundamental review of the way that orders are captured, credit is controlled, production is scheduled and transport is planned. The following four-step procedure can be used to advantage:

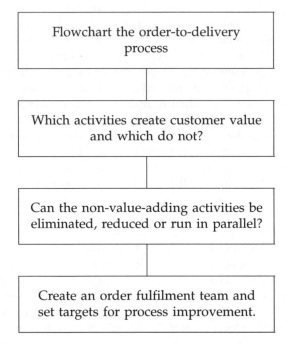

Flowcharting the order-to-delivery process in detail should be the starting point of a time-compression programme. Somehow or another, over the years, most companies have created amazingly complex processes for converting a customer's order into cash. As a business grows in size it might well take on more people in its order entry department. These people then require more supervisors, who have to file more reports. Similarly, as new accounts are gained, changes to the credit control function are made and more activities are likely to be inserted into the routine. Inevitably this adds to the complexity of the process, and these cumbersome processes are further institutionalised through computerisation. Managers are often surprised to be confronted with the results of a flowcharting exercise on, say, order processing. 'Something as simple as processing an order surely cannot involve over 100 separate steps' is a not-untypical response!

To simplify and speed up the order-to-delivery cycle requires a cross-functional approach. A powerful way to achieve significant improvements in this crucial area is through the creation of an order fulfilment team that draws from all the functional activities involved in the chain of events from receipt of order through to final delivery and invoicing. Thus sales order entry, credit control, production planning, transport scheduling and invoicing are all represented on the team. The first priority of the team is to focus on ways in which the entire process can be simplified through the elimination of activities or by running those activities in parallel rather than in series, by reducing paperwork and reports, and by questioning the conventional wisdom of how the business should be run.

Invariably this type of cross-functional analysis will reveal many ways in which order-to-delivery times can be improved. Because these re-engineered systems will often be simpler, they will normally be cheaper to operate and require fewer people to run them.

The order fulfilment team should also form the vehicle for the ongoing processing of orders once the systems have been simplified. In other words, instead of the traditional means of processing orders where the order moves from one department to another, there should be an order fulfilment group working as a cross-functional team to manage the order on an integrated basis, from the capture of that order to the final delivery of the product.

Time to react

Volatile markets have become the norm in many industry sectors. Significant upward and downward changes in demand occur almost unpredictably. Many of these swings are due to competitive actions, some are due to changes in customer taste or fashion, and some are self-inflicted as the result of promotional activity or the like.

Managing logistics in these conditions is not easy, and the likelihood of stock-outs or, conversely, over-stocks increases. A response often heard from managers faced with circumstances such as these is: 'if only we had better forecasts'. The reality is that forecasting technology is as good now as it probably ever will be, and in any case nothing short of a crystal ball will predict short-term demand in wildly fluctuating markets. The real challenge is to seek ways in which we can become less dependent upon the forecast. Outdoor equipment manufacturer Karrimor redesigned its entire organisation and redefined its relationships with its trading partners in a bid to become less forecast-dependent. It gained a significant competitive advantage by becoming the first manufacturer in the outdoor equipment industry to embrace time-based competition.

The reason why so much logistics activity is forecast-dependent is the long lead times. The longer the lead time, the further ahead we

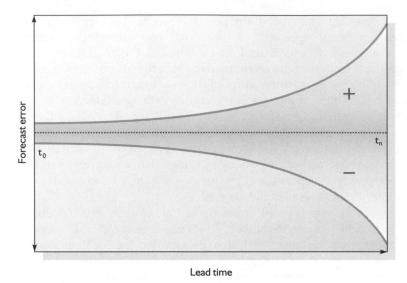

Figure 4.5 Forecast error and lead time

need to forecast. Lead times here refer to the time taken to respond to an upward or a downward change in demand. If there are long replenishment lead times for raw materials or packaging supplies, for example, of necessity we are forced to try to forecast demand over that lead time.

The problem is that forecast accuracy tends to vary directly with lead times. The longer the lead time, the greater the forecast error – indeed the error tends to increase more than proportionately the further ahead we have to forecast, and of course forecast error is one of the major determinants of the need for safety stock. Figure 4.5 shows the effect of lead times on forecast error. One rule of thumb suggests that reducing the lead time by 50 per cent will reduce forecast error by 50 per cent.

Karrimor: rapid response in a seasonal market

Karrimor is a manufacturer of rucksacks and specialist clothing for climbers and hikers. Founded in 1946 by the Parsons family in the small town of Accrington in the North of England, Karrimor started out as a manufacturer of cycle bags but in 1957 switched its focus to rucksacks. During the 1960s and 1970s, close links with leading mountaineers enabled Karrimor to develop its world-renowned range of rugged and well-engineered climbers' rucksacks. However, by the 1980s the company's future looked anything but secure. It was becoming increasingly difficult to protect Karrimor's technological innovations and its market share from a host of 'me-too' competitors.

Realising the danger, Tony Parsons, son of founders Charles and Mary Parsons, began to look for ways to improve Karrimor's competitive position. Joining the British branch of an American businessman's club gave Parsons an opportunity to visit other enterprises and learn from their experience. One in particular, Milliken, the North American textile giant, left a lasting impression. The speed at which Milliken was able to produce goods to order amazed Parsons, and although his own business was tiny by comparison he realised that it too could gain considerable advantage by improving its response times.

With the help of a newly appointed outsider, Tony Cameron, Parsons set about devising a plan to revitalise the business. First, Karrimor was to be the most responsive supplier in its market. Secondly, it would produce a range of patented products to stave off the 'me-too' competition. Thirdly, it would introduce a counter-seasonal garment range to even out cash flow and inventory levels. Finally, it would sell off the old buildings it currently occupied and move to a purpose-built leasehold property nearby. The great advantage of the latter would be that product flows were no longer hampered by production taking place on several floors. Moreover, it would dramatically improve communication between the production and marketing functions, which were previously located in separate buildings.

New equipment was installed, and once the workforce had fully settled into the new site Parsons began channelling his energies into the development of the new garment range. Meanwhile, two new directors were appointed and charged with improving the company's response times and customer relations, and with streamlining the shop floor.

Karrimor and its retailers both suffered from deliveries that were heavily skewed towards the start of the season. Retailers took their entire stock then, which meant that Karrimor had to build up stock ahead of time or attempt to cram as much production as possible through a short delivery window.

Karrimor decided to introduce a new 'StockFlow' system – a simple form of quick response – inviting retailers to place only a small trial order at the beginning of the season. This would be delivered in the normal way, with a tear-off label attached to each item. When an item was sold, the retailer simply returned (or faxed) the label to Karrimor, specifying the quantity required – either a single replacement, or several if the item was selling well.

Retailers were initially reluctant to adopt the system, despite its benefits and simplicity. Larger retailers were unwilling to try new ways of working, and smaller ones looked to them for a lead. In the end a trial was negotiated with a fifteen-outlet chain of stores, committing Karrimor to a 21-day delivery response. The trial was an immediate success, and by 1993 there were 370 outlets using the StockFlow system, which by then handled over 75 per cent of sales.

The StockFlow trial was the first of its kind in the outdoor goods sector. It opened the way for Karrimor's new garment range, speeding market penetration by minimising the risk associated with a brand extension for both supplier and retailer.

Karrimor's manufacturing systems were forced to change as more and more business was called through on quick response. Work-in-progress throughput times were reduced by replacing the factory's piecework payment system with a method that was more conducive to small batch work and less time-consuming to administer.

Sourcing was the next issue to be addressed. A 'supplier day' was held to explain the changes that Karrimor was undertaking. This was quite a departure for a company operating in such a traditional corner of the textile industry, but Karrimor was eager to develop more responsive purchasing to support the quick-response sales and manufacturing systems it had already introduced.

Some suppliers responded well to the call for smaller, more frequent and more reliable deliveries but, where necessary, unresponsive suppliers were replaced. One local supplier of rucksack fabric installed new dyeing vessels, allowing it to produce dyed fabric in smaller batches with faster lead times. The improved supplier-response times allowed Karrimor to change its production planning process. Orders for undyed fabric could be placed with the supplier, but the colour did not have to be confirmed until a later date. If one colour was selling better than another, suppliers' manufacturing schedules could be switched to accommodate demand. Better still, Karrimor could advise retailers to reconsider if they had ordered items in one colour while another colour was enjoying twice the stock-turn.

By 1996 response times for retailers had been reduced to only seven days, and stock had been reduced from £3.6m to £2.1m. Annual sales had reached £20m per annum, with between 35 and 40 per cent of production going for export. By then the thriving business was attracting attention from the international investment community. In October that year the business was acquired by 21 Invest, a venture capital business jointly owned by Italy's famous Benetton and Bonomi families. Karrimor continues to be one of the world's leading outdoor equipment brands.

With the trend towards the globalisation of industry, lead times have if anything tended to lengthen, resulting in longer pipelines with higher levels of variability in total end-to-end time. A further compounding element is that with complex products containing many components or materials, it is the speed of the slowest moving element that determines total pipeline time.

One international brewing company found that the forecast horizon for its West African operation was three months' long – not because it took that long to brew the beer, but because the gold foil that went on top of the bottle could not be sourced locally and had to be procured through its European buying organisation, with a three-month lead time! Not only did this necessitate a three-month forecast of demand for the product, but it also limited flexibility of response. For example, if for some unexpected reason demand for beer were to rise, then the ability to meet that increased demand would be severely impaired.

Many companies have invested great sums in manufacturing automation to speed up throughput times in the factory, but find that because the pipeline as a whole is inflexible they still have problems reacting to demand changes. For example, best practice in the Western European car industry has reduced the time taken to assemble a car to a matter of hours. Yet average inventory of finished products – cars waiting to be sold – is still likely to amount to weeks or even months for many companies. Such stock-mountains not only eat up working capital; they can also constrain companies' ability to meet the precise needs of customers for specific models and options.

What in practice can be done to reduce lead times in a business so that it might simultaneously improve delivery performance and reaction times?

Strategies for lead-time reduction

From the earlier discussion it will be clear that a number of significant benefits can be gained if pipeline time can be reduced. Not only does lead-time reduction free up working capital, it can also enable faster and more flexible response.

The key to unlocking these prizes lies in what might be termed *strategic lead-time management*. To manage lead times strategically requires an understanding of their character. For most products there will not be one lead time but many, as each component that goes into the final product may be subject to different lead times as they move from different suppliers through different supply chains. For most purposes, however, it is sensible to take the slowest moving element in the chain to determine total pipeline length. The approach is a form of *critical path analysis* in that attempts to shorten pipeline time should proceed by working to reduce the longest lead time in the chain until some other element emerges as the critical path, and so on.

To assist in the identification of opportunities for pipeline time reduction, it is helpful to 'map' the pipeline from one end to the other. A pipeline or supply chain map is essentially a time-based representation of the processes that are involved as the materials or products move through the chain. At the same time the map should show the time that is consumed when those materials or products are simply standing still (i.e. as inventory).

In these maps it is useful to distinguish between 'horizontal' time and 'vertical' time. Horizontal time is time spent in process. It could be in-transit time, manufacturing or assembly time, order-processing time

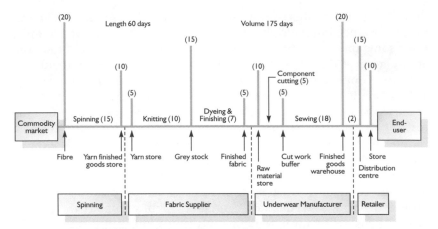

Figure 4.6 Supply chain mapping – an example (*Source*: Westbrook, S., Westbrook, C. and Westbrook, R. (1991) New strategic tools for supply chain management, *International Journal of Physical Distribution and Logistics Management*, 21(1)).

and so on. It may not necessarily be time when customer value is being created, but at least something is going on. The other type of time is vertical time; this is time when nothing is happening, and hence the material or product is standing still as inventory. No value is being added during vertical time, only cost.

The labels 'horizontal' and 'vertical' refer to the maps themselves, where the two axes reflect process time and time spent as static inventory respectively. Figure 4.6 depicts such a map of the manufacture and distribution of men's underwear.

From this map it can be seen that horizontal time is 60 days – in other words, the various processes of gathering materials, spinning, knitting, dyeing, finishing, sewing etc. take 60 days to complete from start to finish. This is important, because horizontal time determines the time that it would take the system to respond to an increase in demand. Hence if there was a sudden upsurge in demand it would take that long to 'ramp-up' output to the new level. Conversely, if there was a downturn in demand then the critical measure would be pipeline volume – i.e. the sum of both horizontal and vertical time. In other words, it would take 175 days to 'drain' the system of inventory. Men's underwear is not itself a particularly volatile category, but in fashion markets, for instance, pipeline volume is a critical determinant of business risk.

Pipeline maps can also provide a useful internal benchmark. Because each day of process time requires a day of inventory to 'cover' that day, then, in an 'ideal' world, the only inventory would be that needed to provide cover during the process lead time. So 60 days' total process time would result in 60 days' inventory. However, in the case highlighted earlier there are actually 175 days of inventory in the pipeline. Clearly, unless the individual processes are highly time-variable, there is more inventory than can be justified.

Mapping pipelines in this way provides a powerful basis for logistics re-engineering projects. Because we have made the total process and its associated inventory transparent, we are now in a much better position to identify opportunities for improvement.

Value-added time/non-value-added time

One of the reasons that logistics pipelines tend to be longer than is justified by the actual manufacturing and transportation time is because so much time is consumed in what we term *non-value-adding* activities. These are activities where, if a way could be found to reduce the time spent on them or even to eliminate them, there would be no noticeable reduction in value from the customer's perspective. If, for example, the time taken to process an order were reduced, then customers would not see this as a reduction in value – indeed, if it meant they got the delivery sooner they might regard it as an improvement. Likewise, a reduction of inventory in a warehouse, as long as it did not lead to more out-of-stock situations, would not reduce customer value although it would most certainly reduce costs.

A good starting point, therefore, for time-compression projects is to analyse the pipeline from start to finish, classifying every step in the

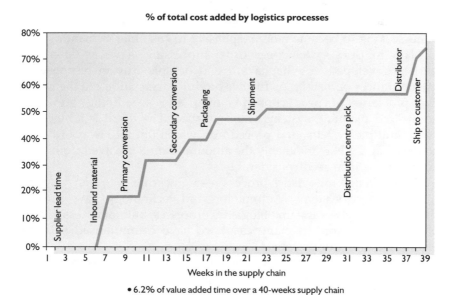

% of total cost added by logistics processes

Weeks in the supply chain

- 6.2% of value added time over a 40-weeks supply chain
- Buffering against business process and variability at each stage – no single buffer is unreasonable

Figure 4.7 Value added through time

chain in terms of whether customer value is being created at that step or merely cost. It can be quite depressing to perform these analyses and to discover that only a small proportion of time in the pipeline is actually spent creating customer value. Figure 4.7 gives an actual example from the pharmaceutical industry.

This is not an extreme case. It is quite common to encounter organisations where less than 10 per cent of total pipeline time is consumed in creating customer value. If anything the problem has been exacerbated by modern manufacturing technology, where automation enables products to be manufactured in ever-shorter timeframes and in greater volumes only for them to sit as finished inventory in a warehouse waiting for demand to catch up with production.

The real focus of logistics process re-engineering should be upon finding ways to reduce the non-value-adding components of total pipeline time. Clearly there may be cost implications that will need to be weighed in the balance, but more often than not speeding up processes actually leads to significant overall cost reduction as well as to a reduction in total system inventory.

Logistics process re-engineering

There has been a tendency by some to see Business Process Re-engineering (BPR) as yet another management fad with a focus primarily on cost and overhead reduction. This is a pity, since the philosophy of BPR, which essentially is about simplification and the reduction of non-value-adding activities, has much to offer organisations seeking to become more responsive to customer demand.

Many logistics systems, e.g. order processing, have, as described earlier, developed in a haphazard and organic way in response to circumstances of history. As further products were added to the range the problems of production planning and scheduling grew, so formalised planning systems were installed. The result is a business with multiple systems and procedures, which do not always fit well together, and where inevitably the amount of time involved from start to finish has increased considerably.

The challenge to logistics process re-engineering is to find ways to simplify these systems. Automation and technology have greatly assisted in the speeding up of logistics processes, but not necessarily in their simplification. In many cases we have computerised existing inefficiencies in our systems.

Elsewhere in the logistics system opportunities for time compression can be found through eliminating stages in a multi-echelon distribution chain. Many companies, particularly in overseas distribution, have traditionally moved inventory from factory through regional distribution centres to national warehouses and even to local stocking points. The original logic for this arrangement was that transport costs could be minimised by shipping in bulk, and that distant markets should maintain inventory to cover against long transit times.

Today's logic might argue much more strongly for making use of direct delivery wherever possible. Intermediate stockholding rarely if ever adds customer value (only if some form of break-bulk activity, packaging or final configuration is involved). Eliminating these steps will reduce total system inventory, handling and warehouse costs, and will of course reduce lead times. Whilst transportation costs might increase, the overall benefit from both service and cost points of view will be positive.

Re-engineering the flow of information from the market place to the supplier and beyond can have a profound effect on responsiveness. Improving the visibility of real demand up and down the supply chain allows each party in that chain to anticipate demand better. This is a theme that will be dealt with further in Chapter 5.

For most businesses, demand information is hidden by intermediate inventories in the form of distribution centres and warehouses. Even though those stocking points may be essential to the efficient physical flow of product, they should not be allowed to act as filters of information on real demand. Likewise, when orders are transmitted back from one stage in the chain to another, great benefit could be gained if the order could distinguish between that part of it used to replenish depleted inventory and that part which reflects an increase in real demand.

Speeding up the flow of information and relating it more directly to real movements in market-place demand can do more to enable a business to become a time-based competitor than almost anything else. Because most companies have a 'lead-time gap' (i.e. the total pipeline time is greater than the customer's willingness to wait), information must be used to close the gap. If relevant information cannot be made available, the logistics network will have no choice but to depend upon inventory to service customers, with all the attendant problems that brings. Figure 4.8 illustrates the lead-time gap.

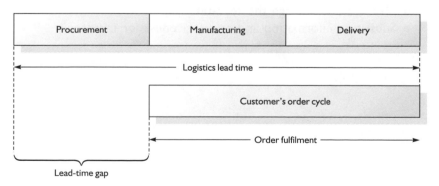

Figure 4.8 The lead-time gap

The key to reducing the lead-time gap lies not only in reducing total pipeline time, but also in gaining earlier warning of customer requirements. The latter is achieved through establishing better communication with customers and, ideally, by getting as close as possible to 'real-time' demand. In other words, if what is happening in the final market place could be communicated as far as possible up the supply chain as and when it happens, then all parties in that chain could move much closer to a just-in-time response.

Time-based competition is now widely accepted as a powerful basis for gaining advantage in volatile markets and in an environment characterised by shortening product life cycles. Not every product or every market requires a just-in-time strategy, and the costs of time compression may not always justify the benefits. However, the more demanding the customer becomes and the more the competitive pressure intensifies, almost inevitably the prizes will go to the more responsive organisation.

Time-based competition: key issues

■ Time becomes a critical source of competitive advantage
  ● The cash-to-cash cycle and end-to-end pipeline time
  ● Reducing time to market, time to serve and time to react
  ● Shorter pipelines provide greater flexibility at less cost

■ Strategies for lead-time reduction
  ● Pipeline mapping as a means of focusing improvement activities
  ● The difference between value-adding time and non-value-adding time

■ Logistics process re-engineering
  ● Understand and simplify logistics processes
  ● Measure and manage the 'lead-time gap'
  ● Substitute information and responsiveness for inventory

Chapter 5

Demand-driven supply chains

'Matching supply with demand' is the fundamental goal of the logistics process. Conventional business practice seeks to mediate demand and supply through forecasts – in other words, the forecast is used as an attempt to predict demand and then finished goods inventory is created ahead of that anticipated demand. However, because today's market place is considerably more volatile and, as a result, less predictable, it has become necessary to seek alternative approaches to demand management. The way forward is to substitute information for inventory and in the process become more responsive to real demand. Becoming demand-driven requires a supply chain that is 'agile' in its ability to meet changed customer requirements. New ways of working with supply chain partners are required if customer responsiveness is to be enhanced.

Today's market place is characterised by a much higher level of turbulence than has previously been the case. Markets have fragmented, and customers and consumers require customised solutions; the days of standard products made ahead of demand for mass markets have long gone. In a world such as this, traditional approaches to forecast-based management become increasingly untenable. The reason for this is that classic statistical forecasting is often based upon taking information on past demand and then trying to identify patterns from which projections into the future can be made. However, when previous sales show no patterns because of volatile shifts in demand, then clearly there is no basis for a forecast.

Capturing information on the requirements of customers or consumers as close as possible to the point of sale or point of use should be a key goal of supply chain management. However, many organisations are forced to anticipate those requirements through a forecast since they have no clear view of the final market place. Thus the supplier of packaging material to a chocolate manufacturer may not see anything other than the orders it receives from the chocolate company. Similarly, the chocolate company will probably not see the real consumer demand off the shelf at the retailer, if the retailer only sends sporadic orders. In most supply chains the majority of manufacturing and distribution activities are driven by a forecast rather than by demand.

The point at which activities cease to be forecast-driven and become demand-driven has been termed the 'order penetration point', although the term 'demand penetration point' is more accurate. All the activities upstream of the demand penetration point are forecast-driven, with all the consequent problems that that can bring.

The challenge to the supply chain is to find ways in which the demand penetration point can be pushed as far upstream as possible. Through sharing information on real demand it becomes possible for supply chain partners to synchronise their operations and become more in line with the needs of the market place. At the same time as moving the demand penetration point upstream, the aim should be to move the 'decoupling point' as far as possible downstream. The decoupling point is, in effect, the point of commitment – the moment where inventory, held in a generic form, is committed to a particular finished form or to specific customers or markets.

The decoupling point represents the transition from forecast-driven activities to demand-driven activities. Figure 5.1 shows different situations, ranging from a 'make-to-order' environment (where demand penetrates to the far end of the chain) to the more commonly encountered situation where only the last party in the chain interfacing with the consumer actually experiences real demand.

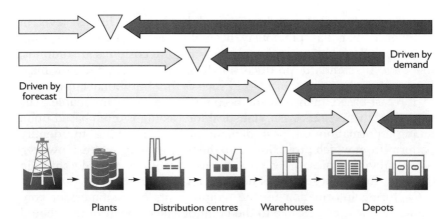

Figure 5.1 The demand penetration point

There was a time, of course, when make-to-order was the norm in almost every industry, but industrialisation brought mass production and with it greater uniformity and lower costs through economies of scale. Thereafter, make-to-order tended to occupy high-value, low-volume niches far removed from the everyday mass market. In consumer goods terms, these products would likely be luxury goods or the outputs of craft industries. In recent years, however, advances in manufacturing and information technology have made make-to-order an affordable option even for FMCG goods.

In certain circumstances flexible manufacturing and logistics systems can allow manufacturers to reduce work-in-progress, all but eliminate finished goods inventory, *and* create additional value for their customers by making each and every product to a bespoke customer order. This is 'mass customisation'.

Mass customisation

According to Professor Paul Zipkin of Duke University in the USA, mass customisation is 'mass production with variety'. For the customer, the upside of this value proposition is that the products are tailored to meet his or her particular requirements. The downside is that the customer is likely to have to wait to get them.

Mass-customisation systems must have three key capabilities: elicitation; process flexibility and responsive logistics (Zipkin, P. (2001) The limits of mass customisation, *MIT Sloan Management Review*, Spring, 81–86). All three must themselves be bound together by effective communication systems capable of tracking a discrete customer order from elicitation through to final delivery.

Elicitation requires a mechanism for interacting with customers and obtaining specific information. An elicitation process must provide a simple and user-friendly means of leading customers through the process of identifying their exact requirements. It must capture identification details, such as name and address; customers' selections from menus of alternatives; physical measurements/quantity; and reactions to prototypes. In some instances the customer's requirements may be as simple to elicit as a name or a message to be featured on the finished goods, or perhaps a series of easy-to-obtain measurements to determine the dimensions of the finished item. The example of Reflect.com, presented here, is one of the more unusual examples in that the selection process seeks to elicit highly esoteric requirements.

Process flexibility is the second essential requirement. Some industries have progressed further than others; customisation may only be possible in one or two processing phases. In engineering and the apparel industry, mass-production systems have been made more flexible though CAD/CAM systems, modular design and the wider use of digitally controlled manufacturing equipment.

The third key capability is responsive logistics systems in terms of further processing if the customisation stage is not performed at the final step in the production process, plus of course distribution. This stage may involve localisation of packing and tailored service packages, for example.

Mass customisation at Reflect.com

Reflect.com is one of several specialist beauty products sites that sprang up on the crest of the dot.com wave. The company was founded in September 1999 with a $50 million investment from Procter & Gamble, its majority share-holder. Unlike a number of its competitors, it survived the first big shake out of the dot.com industry. Other start-ups crashed and burned after being unable to secure inventory, deliver on time, or keep pace with changing consumer trends.

P&G was a willing backer of the business, which offers beauty products designed and blended to meet the specific preferences of individual consumers. The product range includes cosmetics, skincare, shampoos, and even a fragrance brand called 'Hearts and Souls'. The Hearts and Souls process allows customers to create their very own signature scent by responding on-line to a series of questions and assessing a number of visual images.

For the customer, the process of capturing the essence of herself in a scent begins with deciding when she is most likely to wear the fragrance (daytime, evening, special events) and what kind of a mood she is seeking to evoke (e.g. modern, classic, sporty). After defining those she is invited to choose a number of 'visuals' from ranges of photographic images on the basis of which one appeals most to her senses. The on-line profile determines the combinations of essential oils and other ingredients to be used.

For $5, Reflect will blend and ship three samples based on the customer's 'Hearts and Souls' selection. She is under no further obligation to buy, but should she choose to purchase one of the scents the $5 fee is off-set against the $40 purchase. If none of the samples meet with her requirements, the customer can expect a full refund without having to return the unsatisfactory items. Alternatively, she can repeat the process and will receive a batch of 'recustomised' samples at no further cost.

Most customers choose a name for their fragrance, which the company engraves on the container free of charge. Shipping is also free of charge, and delivery is approximately ten days after the on-line order placement.

Postponement

An alternative to all-out mass customisation is 'postponement'. This also delivers variety while retaining the cost-efficiencies of mass production, this time by changing the sequence of activities in the manufacturing and logistics processes. It postpones the point at which work-in-progress is committed to become a specific variant of an otherwise standard finished product.

Postponement reduces forecasting risk by carrying inventory in a generic or unfinished form, delaying final product configuration until actual demand is known. Final configuration may mean final assembly, finishing, colouring or packaging, depending on the type of product in question. The benefit of postponement is that the total inventory holding within the system is lowered and, because the inventory is generic, the risk of over-stocking (or indeed under-stocking) is reduced. At the same time choice is enhanced and so is customer service. The customer may have to wait for the finished product, but the lead time is unlikely to be as long as if the item had been produced to order from scratch.

So, for example, office equipment manufacturer Xerox endeavours not to hold any product as fully finished inventory. Instead it will carry inventory as work-in-progress, in modular, semi-finished form, and will then configure the final product only when an order is received.

Another example is household paint mixed to the required colour in DIY stores. ICI Paint's 'Dulux Colour Mixing System' delays the point of commitment to a particular colour until it reaches the final point of sale. Inventory is supplied to the stores ready packaged in a number of standard volume units (i.e. tins) of neutral base. The resealable packaging is opened to allow pigment to be added as and when required by a customer at the point of sale.

Creating 'agile' supply chains

In complex supply chains the only way that the demand penetration point can be moved upstream, or indeed that the point of commitment can be moved closer to the point of sale, is by collaboration between supply chain partners – in particular, collaboration through the sharing of information.

One of the fundamental drivers of supply chain integration is the realisation that 'agility' is a vital prerequisite for market responsiveness. Traditional inventory-based systems that sought to anticipate customer requirements through sales forecasts have been challenged by the advent of just-in-time, quick response solutions that rely on information rather than inventory to meet customers' needs. 'Substituting information for inventory' has become the guiding principle for logistics managers in those organisations that seek to achieve flexible and timely response in volatile and short life-cycle markets.

As conventional supply chains comprise separate corporate entities with only minimal upstream and downstream transparency of market-related information, they buffer themselves against uncertainty of demand by holding inventory. As a result these supply chains carry inventory far in excess of current requirements, with duplication of stock at each buyer–supplier interface. Not only is this a significant burden in terms of working capital but, even more importantly, such chains are slow to respond to volatile demand. An analogy can be drawn with an oil pipeline that is lengthy and slow moving and in which the oil must pass through many intermediate storage tanks before finally reaching the end market. If the customers' requirements for the type and grade of oil were to change frequently, the supplying company would face significant problems in meeting those requirements.

A further problem with supply chains with numerous buffers between the two ends of the chain is that small changes in demand in the final market place are amplified and distorted as they move back through the chain. This is the well-known 'bull-whip' or 'Forrester' effect (named after the professor from Massachusetts Institute of Technology who first identified it), which is the cause of considerable hidden cost to the supply chain as a whole.

The Forrester effect has its roots in the fact that in a chain of several players, each acting independently of each other and probably only sharing minimal (if any) information, the likelihood is that even small changes in end-user demand will result in amplified demand the further upstream the surge travels. The causes of this 'tidal wave' or 'bull-whip' phenomenon are based primarily on the fact that independent inventories at each step in the chain act as buffers that distort and amplify requirements and in effect 'hide' real demand from upstream suppliers.

Let us take a simple example. Market research suggests that the cat owners of the United Kingdom who buy tinned cat food feed their cats about the same amount every day. However, most of these cat owners do not buy in single cans but in multiples, with a delay between purchase occasions. Similarly, the retail store at which they buy these products orders by the pallet load or even the truckload, again at varying frequencies. Other distribution channels, such as wholesalers and cash and carry, will also be ordering according to their own re-order level policies, and of course significant promotional activity will be taking place almost continuously, creating temporary brand switching amongst cat owners and/or forward buying by retailers and wholesalers.

The combined effect of all of this is to create a very volatile picture of demand by the time this filtered and distorted picture is received at the cat food factory! And of course things become even more distorted as these demands are translated into upstream requirements for raw materials, packaging products and so on.

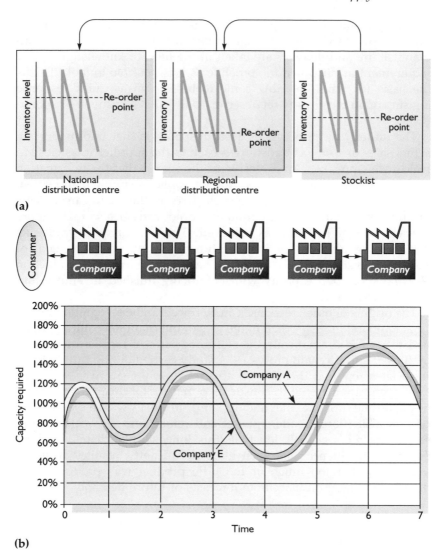

(a)

(b)

Figure 5.2 (a) Inventory hides demand; (b) Supply chain interactions cause upstream fluctuations

Figure 5.2(a) demonstrates how, at each stage in the chain, inventory first hides demand and then leads to a 'lumpy' and lagged order on the next upstream party in the chain. Figure 5.2(b) illustrates how small changes in demand in the end-user market can create significant oscillations the further up the chain we go.

To combat these inefficiencies in the supply chain, new style relationships are emerging between the entities in the chain based upon a more open sharing of information. Instead of supply chain members having to anticipate requirements on the basis of forecasts, the aim now is to become *demand-driven* – in other words, decisions on manufacture and delivery are taken in the light of knowledge of real requirement as far down the pipeline as it is possible to look. This is the basis for what has now come to be known as quick response logistics or, in the grocery retail sector, as Efficient Consumer Response (ECR).

The underlying principle of quick response is that information on actual sales or usage is transmitted back to the supplier in as close to real time as possible. An extension of the idea is that the information is also shared simultaneously with the supplier's supplier, and so on. On the basis of this information each party in the chain can manage production, assembly, distribution and other activities so that a more efficient use of resources is achieved. This may require trade-offs between organisations or internal functional interests. The goal of quick response logistics is therefore better overall use of production and transportation capacity whilst reducing finished inventory and working capital.

The origins of quick response can be traced to the recognition by the USA's apparel industry that, in the face of international competition, it had to reduce dramatically the self-imposed cost burden of its own inefficient supply chain processes. A study carried out by Kurt Salmon Associates reported that the US apparel supply chain was 66 weeks long from raw material to consumer purchase. Of this, 11 weeks was in-plant time (fibre, textiles and apparel), 40 weeks was in warehouses or in transit (fibre, textile, apparel and retail), and 15 weeks was in store. The report concluded that 'this long supply chain was both expensive to finance and, even more significantly, resulted in major losses as either too much or too little product was produced and distributed based on inaccurate forecasts of future demand'.

Banding together with Milliken

In 1981, US textile and apparel producers enjoyed an 80 per cent share of their domestic market. Six years later, their share was 60 per cent. Protectionist legislation slowed this decline, but profits went in to freefall at the end of the 1980s, plunging from $1.9 billion in 1987 to $600 million in 1991.

Searching for a competitive advantage, US industry leaders appealed to the patriotism of American consumers, forming the 'Crafted with Pride in the USA Council Inc.' The Council's 500 members funded a $100 million advertising programme to promote American-made clothing, but discovered that when it came to value-for-money clothing, American consumers were not that patriotic. Their next reaction was for the stronger parties in a supply chain to shift the burden of inventory to weaker players. This did not work either, because the disconnected and often adversarial supply chains were still slow, costly and ineffective.

Beyond the style-setting international couturiers, the critical success factors in the apparel industry are the ability to spot what will sell and then to get it into the shops first. In both respects, the US-based manufacturers were losing out badly to the likes of Italian fashion group Benetton, and the Far Eastern suppliers of successful niche retailers like The Limited and The Gap. The Council realised that efficiency and consumer responsiveness were the industry's best defence. The indigenous apparel industry could not compete on labour costs, but distance was in its favour. It should be able to compete in its own market by virtue of location, on time and transport costs.

The Council commissioned consultants Kurt Salmon Associates to study US apparel industry supply chains. The results were alarming. The supply chains were too long and too badly co-ordinated to respond effectively to market-place demands. Time to market averaged one and a quarter years from textile loom to store rack. Industry-wide, the cost of this inefficiency was estimated to be approximately $25 billion per year – around 20 per cent of the industry's total turnover. The supply chain could not absorb these costs, so they were passed on to the customer – until imports became a threat.

The US industry had to find new ways of working if it was going to survive. Several pilot studies were therefore commissioned to see if pipelines could be shortened by collaboration between retailers, apparel manufactures and textile producers. Among the first to participate in the pilot studies was Milliken & Co., the country's largest textile producer.

Prior to this experiment the order fulfilment process was as follows: Milliken received incoming orders – slowly – by US mail. Weaving would normally be completed eight weeks after the yarn became available. Dyeing and finishing took a further four to five weeks, and the stock would then be forwarded to the central warehouse until required by the customer. Keeping the factory operating at maximum capacity was the overriding priority.

After Milliken, an apparel manufacturer could take around eighteen to twenty weeks from receipt of cloth to delivering the clothing to a retailer. The retailers, fearing stock-outs, regularly over ordered, increasing their carrying costs and resulting in markdowns of excess stock. If the retailer's inventories become too high they would cut back on purchasing, leaving the manu-facturers with excess stock. They in turn would cancel fabric orders, leaving Milliken holding unwanted inventory at its own cost.

In the pilot study, Milliken partnered with apparel manufacturer Seminole, and with Wal-Mart stores. Consultants monitored a single product line (basic slacks), measuring the sales and profit improvement delivered by the implementation of quick response. The results showed increased sales of 31 per cent, and a 30 per cent improvement in inventory turns.

The exercise taught Milliken to look beyond its immediate customer – the apparel producer who paid the fabric invoice – so as to be responsive to the end consumers' requirements. If point-of-sale information could be shared between the partners, long-range forecasting and overstocking and order cancellations would no longer be necessary. Milliken began seeking out like-minded supply-chain partners who were willing to set aside short-term self-interest to create integrated supply chains.

The lessons learned in the apparel industry were used to improve other areas of Milliken's textile business. For example, the company approached one of its customers, a retailer of oriental-style rugs, with an offer to manufacture the rugs to order by quick response, then ship them by UPS direct to the customer's home. The retailer would, however, have to forward its customer orders to Milliken on a daily basis, and keep it fully informed of planned promotional activity. The retailer hesitated at first, but then agreed. The move allowed the retailer to eliminate its entire inventory of the product, keeping only display items, while cutting delivery times and costs because the rugs no longer passed through its distribution centre.

Connecting the supply chain through shared information

A number of industry-wide initiatives in the US apparel business have led to increasing supply chain collaboration in order to speed up the flow of information through the chain, and hence its responsiveness. Essentially what has happened is that information from the retail checkout counter through electronic point of sale (EPOS) data is transmitted back to the apparel manufacturer, from there to the upstream fabric maker and beyond that to the fibre manufacturer. Figure 5.3 summarises the process.

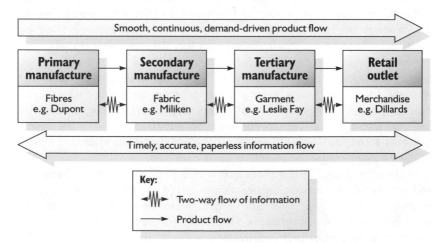

Figure 5.3 Quick response in the US apparel industry (*Source*: Kurt Salmon Associates)

It is clear that information technology plays a significant role in making quick response possible, but it should be seen more as an enabler rather than a primary driver. The real prerequisite for quick response is a reorientation of the supply chain towards co-operation through shared information.

In many other sectors of industry, supply chain collaboration and data sharing first emerged in the form of Vendor Managed Inventory (VMI) programmes. VMI is a process through which the supplier manages the flow of product into the customer's manufacturing or distribution system. This flow is determined by frequent exchanges of information about the actual off-take or usage of the product at the level of the customer. With this information the supplier is able to take account of current inventories at each level in the chain, as well as goods in transit, when determining what quantity to ship and when to ship it. The supplier is in effect managing the customer's inventory on the customer's behalf. In a VMI environment there are no customer orders; instead the supplier makes decisions on shipping quantities based upon the information it receives direct from point of use or the point of sale, or more usually from off-take data at the customers' distribution centre. The supplier can use this information to forecast future requirements and hence to utilise their own production and logistics capacity better.

VMI programmes typically involve a few high-volume Stock-Keeping Units (SKUs), and work well where demand is relatively stable. In the European petrochemical industry, for example, suppliers use remote monitoring of customer inventories of certain bulk liquid products and are thus able to identify when replenishment delivery needs to be made. Similarly, petrol suppliers to retail petrol stations can monitor remotely the sales of each grade of fuel and plan their deliveries accordingly.

In the FMCG sector US-based retailer Wal-Mart, working with one of its most sophisticated branded goods suppliers, Procter & Gamble (P&G), pioneered more radical supply chain management collaborations based directly on point of sale (POS) data. P&G first established a successful VMI programme with Wal-Mart, whereby it was given access to the retailer's daily warehouse shipment data in order to manage the flow of 'Pampers' (disposable nappies) into Wal-Mart's distribution centres.

Wal-Mart went on to offer P&G direct access to POS data, enabling P&G to reduce costs and improve efficiency further by delivering on a just-in-time basis. To stabilise demand enough for just-in-time to be viable, promotionally-induced fluctuations were eliminated by the adoption of an 'everyday low pricing' strategy between Wal-Mart and P&G. Thus the trading partners effected the continuous replenishment of disposable nappies, and then extended the pilot to other high volume items. In this instance the data were exchanged first by fax and telephone, and later through satellite-based Electronic Data Inter-change (EDI).

Earlier warnings of the requirements enable P&G to schedule delivery better and to determine production plans. Sharing the demand data with its own suppliers has also allowed it to plan its own production and material requirements with its suppliers. Furthermore, where it operates in a collaborative data sharing environment P&G report significant improvements in retailer stock-turn on their prod-ucts. Stock-turns of 100+ per cent on the retail shelf are not usual. In the USA these performance improvements opened the way for P&G to play a more active role in category management.

One further benefit to the customer of VMI is that it can be extended into the payment system. Under such a regime, the customer receives stocks on 'consignment', paying the supplier for the product only when it is used or sold. The impact on the customer's cash flow can be dramatic.

Following on the heels of the P&G–Wal-Mart collaboration, and the success of quick response in the apparel industry, came the Efficient Consumer Response (ECR) movement.

Efficient consumer response

ECR was launched as a logistics management concept by Kurt Salmon Associates in 1992, from a study of supply chain management in grocery retailing commissioned by the US Food Marketing Institute. In essence, ECR takes the principles of demand-driven logistics, devel-oped in the motor manufacturing and apparel industries under the banners of just-in-time and quick response, and applies them to the distribution of grocery products. ECR encompasses both supply and demand side management techniques. On the supply side it is concerned with the mechanics of supplier integration, where its remit extends from improved forecasting, through sales-based ordering, to cross-docking and the introduction of continuous replenishment or its derivatives, VMI and CMI. CMI refers to Co-Managed Inventory, a variation of VMI, where the purchasing organisation retains some involvement in aspects of the planning and inventory management process. On the demand side, ECR covers new product development and introductions, trade and consumer promotions and all aspects of category management, including product ranging and store assort-ment. Figure 5.4 shows the 'four pillars of ECR', representing four major value-adding supply chain processes and the objectives of each.

The ECR concept formally crossed the Atlantic in the mid-1990s, when the ECR Europe group was formed 'to provide European consumers with the best possible value, service and variety of products

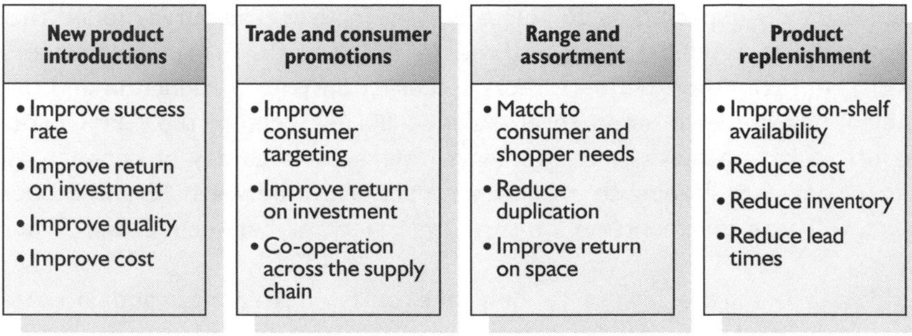

New product introductions	Trade and consumer promotions	Range and assortment	Product replenishment
• Improve success rate • Improve return on investment • Improve quality • Improve cost	• Improve consumer targeting • Improve return on investment • Co-operation across the supply chain	• Match to consumer and shopper needs • Reduce duplication • Improve return on space	• Improve on-shelf availability • Reduce cost • Reduce inventory • Reduce lead times

Figure 5.4 The four pillars of ECR (*Source*: ECR UK Strategy Group)

through a collaborative approach to improving the supply chain' (ECR Europe (1997) *Efficient Consumer Response: Working Together for Total Consumer Satisfaction*, p. 11). Research by a consortium of European manufacturers and retailers led by Coca-Cola had already pronounced that the adoption of quick response principles based upon the sharing of sales data from the point of sale could lead to cost savings amounting to an additional profit opportunity of between 2.3 and 3.4 percentage points of sales turnover at retail prices. The benefits, it proposed, would be split between retailers (approximately 60 per cent) and suppliers (approximately 40 per cent). Later studies undertaken for the ECR Europe consortium indicated that industry-wide cost savings of up to $33 billion per annum could be realised if ECR techniques were to be adopted across the sector.

Despite the efforts of ECR Europe, ECR principles have not been implemented as widely or as quickly as its early advocates had hoped. The number of organisations, large and small, engaging in a formalised efficiency-enhancing approach to CMI – known as Collaborative Planning, Forecasting and Replenishment (CPFR) – has gradually increased.

CPFR in Europe

In 2001, a survey by management consultants Accenture for ECR Europe found that most CPFR initiatives remain one-to-one pilots between retailers and manufacturers. Only one in five of these CPFR pilot programmes had even attempted to integrate data directly from POS. Most used off-take data from the distribution centre or POS data aggregated to that level, as systems integration and high volume data handling problems often emerge.

The purpose of the CPFR pilots is to test the processes and enabling IT solutions. They last for an average of ten months, with many taking longer than originally expected to complete their objectives. The survey found that pilot projects tended to select three to five Key Performance Indicators (KPIs), with three of them – forecast accuracy, inventory reduction and on-shelf availability – common to all. Around 80 per cent of the CPFR pilots report to have achieved improvements in forecast accuracy of between 10 and 20 per cent, leading to inventory reductions of between 12 and 28 per cent, with improvements of on-shelf availability of between 2 and 9 per cent.

Most pilots were limited to only one or two categories, and involved between 20 and 160 stock-keeping units (SKUs). Fifty-five SKUs were deemed to be around the optimum number for a pilot; any higher than that and the number of manual interventions required was likely to become unmanageable. The complexity of the task and the reported immaturity of available IT solutions were found to have inhibited the scaling up of CPFR beyond pilots and its incorporation into standard operating procedures.

(Source: ECR Europe/Accenture (2002) *European CPFR Insights.*)

ECR Europe has provided a number of useful pointers to others who are about to embark on CPFR programmes of their own. First, CPFR should be undertaken within an existing, working trading relationship, where both parties are accustomed to co-operation in their working environment. A well-established co-operative relationship is likely to ease the way at every step of the process, not least in the task of defining roles within the collaboration processes. Internally, staff should be familiar with the objectives and requirements of collaborative projects. The need for staff training should not be overlooked or underestimated – particularly training for end-users of IT solutions.

A nine-step generic CPFR process model developed by non-profit organisation VICS (Voluntary Inter-industry Commerce Standards) provides a framework for collaboration. The framework is likely to require adjustments to meet the specific needs and circumstances of the participating organisations. Figure 5.5 shows a simplified version of the model.

The demands and resource requirements of CPFR mean that those undertaking pilots are likely to choose to go for 'quick-wins' to establish wider business buy-in. CPFR programmes are unlikely to show improvement in performance for high-volume, frequently purchased everyday products. Demand for these tends to be stable, and in a situation where both parties have a high level of market knowledge and experience CPFR is unlikely to bring any significant improvement over the existing forecasting process. Pilot programmes wishing to demonstrate the real potential of CPFR should focus instead on the management of promotional/seasonal items.

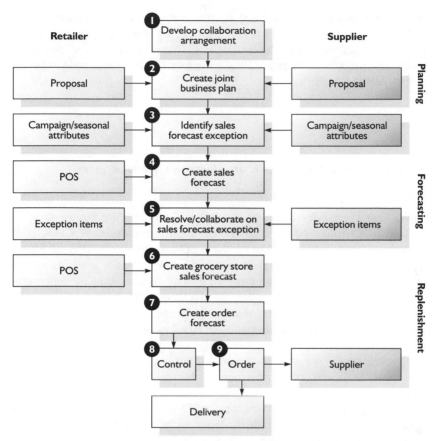

Figure 5.5 VICS-ECR nine-step CPFR model (*Source*: Ketjuetu and Valio/ ECR Europe/Accenture (2002) European CPFR Insights)

Forecasting of promotional sales can be improved dramatically through collaboration, particularly when historical data for similar events are factored in for consideration. Forecasting of new product introductions is particularly difficult because it usually proceeds without the advantage of a basis for comparison, and so demands even greater collaboration, information sharing and resources.

Moving beyond individual pilot programmes, the existence of cultural as well as structural barriers is believed to be inhibiting the implementation of CPFR and indeed the adoption of the ECR principles. Since its migration over the Atlantic in the mid-1990s, many writers have pointed to significant differences between the US and European trading environments. Variations also exist within Europe, with northern European grocers (led by the UK) generally being far more open to the concepts than their counterparts in the southern European states. That is not to say that such initiatives do not or cannot thrive in southern Europe, or that those reported are less sophisticated than the initiatives under way in the northern states, as the one-to-many CPFR example of the Veropoulos Group from Greece illustrates.

Veropoulas – CPFR through an electronic market place

Hellas Spar Veropoulas S.A. (Veropoulas) is Greece's third largest grocery retailer. In October 2001, it embarked upon a one-to-many CPFR pilot with three of its suppliers. Two of the suppliers, Procter & Gamble Hellas and Unilever Hellas S.A., supplied personal and home care products to the retailer. The third, Elgeka, is an integrated retail services supplier representing many branded goods suppliers in the Greek market. Its commercial services offer includes sales, marketing, trade marketing, logistics and merchandising, financial services and information technology.

The other player in the pilot was ONIA-NET, a business start-up seeking to develop, implement and run innovative business solutions in the grocery retail market. It acts as an intermediary between supermarkets and their suppliers, supporting their business transactions and exchange of information via its B2B electronic market place. ONIA-NET offers its partners a collaborative store-ordering model supported by the daily exchange of POS data between retailer and goods suppliers.

The first stage CPFR pilot between the five collaborators lasted three months. It focused on store-level collaboration, the critical interface between the grocery supply chain and the end customer. This is where most of the opportunities for improvement could be expected regarding on-shelf availability. It aimed to do so without inflating overall inventory levels by providing Internet-based daily updates of the full-store situation, from specific store assortment to sell-out data, stock levels in store, information on promotions and out-of-shelf notifications.

The group objectives for the CPFR pilot were stated as follows:

- Eliminate supply chain inefficiencies through collaboration between trading partners by daily exchange of POS data and other critical information at a store level
- Improve on-shelf availability and better fulfil consumer needs
- Reduce inventory levels at store level as well as at the central warehouse
- Optimise the ordering process by eliminating inefficiencies, decreasing costs and increasing job satisfaction

- Improve the process of promotion management and evaluation through sharing and jointly monitoring promotional plans
- Assess the value of working in collaboration over the ONIA-NET platform in a many-to-many (initially one-to-many) environment based on the Process of Collaborative Store Ordering (PCSO™).

An important facilitator for the project was that the ONIA-NET platform provided a common communications platform between the suppliers' offices and the stores. Data shared between partners included catalogue data, assortment data, daily POS data, order proposal, final orders sent by the buyer, information on order fulfilment, out-of-shelf alerts and promotional plans. The information flows were vertical between retailer and supplier. There was no collaboration or data exchange between companies at the same level in the value chain.

The scope of the pilot included ten representative stores, from convenience stores to hypermarkets (five as pilot stores integrated within the collaborative system and five as control stores). Replenishment covered both direct-to-store deliveries and those via a central warehouse.

The key participants within the organisations were the store manager and the suppliers' salesmen; the latter were to be allowed to place a proposed order independently. Personnel within the central retailer and supplier offices also played a part.

The partners spent some time developing a prototype of the PCSO™ that integrated the needs of each of the participating companies. New internal and external processes were designed, and the supporting system continued to develop until one month before the CPFR trial went live, when staff training began.

On-shelf availability was calculated through random daily store visits and on-shelf checks by researchers, who investigated reasons behind any out-of-shelf situations as they arose. Measurements were made during the two weeks before the pilot, over one week in the middle, and for one week at the end. Analysis of the pre-pilot data showed that around 70 per cent of the out-of-shelf was attributable to wrong order quantity or no order at all (see Figure 5.6). These results were compared to post-pilot situations and between pilot and control stores (see Figure 5.7). The results showed a marked decrease in the number of out-of-shelf situations for the pilot sites. Importantly, while stock-outs decreased, inventory levels at these stores also decreased – more so than in control stores.

Further pilot phases were to follow that would extend the pilot to incorporate more SKUs and further KPIs. However, Veropoulos had already declared its intent to extend the implementation of the ONIA-NET PCSO™ system through its entire chain, with new suppliers and possibly other retailers gradually joining the CPFR process through the market place.

(Source: ECR Europe (2002) *European CPFR Insights*.)

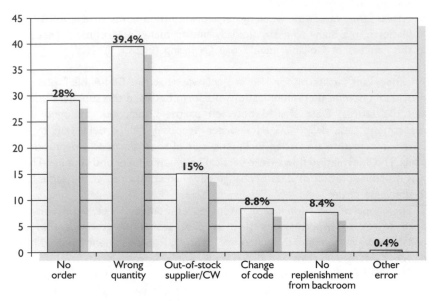

Figure 5.6 Reasons for out-of-shelf before CPFR pilot

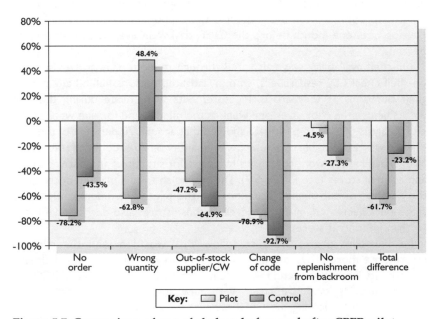

Figure 5.7 Comparison of out-of-shelves before and after CPFR pilot

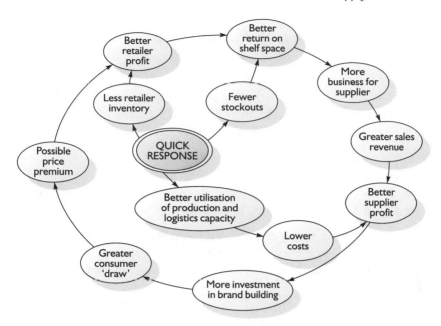

Figure 5.8 Creating a virtuous circle through quick response

The one-to-many web-based model of the Veropoulas case, whilst still focusing on efficiency and improved customer and consumer service through better on-shelf availability, takes the participants a step closer than many CPFR pilots to establishing an infrastructure that could facilitate the management of the demand-side goals of ECR. These are of course the areas where the competing interests of supply chain efficiency collide with marketing's desire to stimulate demand. Category management straddles this fault-line, and is the subject of further discussion in Chapter 6.

In summary, this chapter has explained how demand-driven logistics and ECR in particular aim to deliver multiple benefits across the supply chain. Figure 5.8 shows the virtuous circle through which quick response can lower suppliers' costs and so enable them to invest more in building the brand through innovation and classic marketing. Although sometimes difficult and always resource-intensive to establish, if effective such a programme can even justify a price premium. At the same time, the customer benefits through lower inventory with fewer stock-outs. If the customer is a retailer or distributor it will also achieve a better return on shelf space, and thus will be inclined to give more business to the supplier. In other words, a virtuous circle is created with continuing benefits to both the supplier and the customer.

Demand-driven supply chains: key issues

- Coping with volatile demand
  - Shift the demand penetration point further upstream
  - Utilise mass-customisation strategies
  - Explore opportunities for postponement

- Creating agile supply chains
  - Inventory hides demand
  - Distortions in demand created through the 'bull-whip' effect
  - Quick response is driven by information on real demand

- Connecting the supply chain through shared information
  - Supply chain collaboration enables quick response
  - Efficient consumer response provides a platform for buyer–seller collaboration
  - Collaborative planning, forecasting and replenishment brings supply chain integration closer

Chapter 6

Managing marketing logistics

Most managers work in organisations that are structured as departmental/functional hierarchies. The organisation chart for the archetypal company resembles a pyramid. It provides a clear view of where everyone fits in relation to each other in terms of reporting relationships. In essence, this conventional organisation structure is little changed since the armies of the Roman Empire developed the precursor of today's organisation.

Whilst there can be no doubt that this organisational model has served us well in the past, there are now serious questions regarding its appropriateness for the changed conditions that confront us today. Of the many changes that have taken place in the marketing environment, perhaps the biggest is the focus upon 'speed'. Because of shortening product life cycles, time to market becomes ever more critical. Similarly, the dramatic growth of just-in-time practices means that those companies wishing to supply into those types of environment have to develop systems capable of responding rapidly and flexibly to customers' delivery requirements.

The challenge to every business is to become a *responsive organisation* in every sense of the word. The organisation must respond to changes in the market with products and services that provide innovative solutions to customers' problems; it must be capable of responding to volatile demand and able to provide high levels of flexibility in delivery.

What are the distinguishing characteristics of the responsive organisation? One thing is certain: it does not resemble yesterday's functionally focused business. There are likely to be many differences, but the major transformations will probably be:

- From functions to processes
- From products to customers
- From profit to performance.

From functions to processes

Conventionally, organisations have been functional and hierarchical in their design – in other words, businesses have organised around functions such as production, marketing, sales and distribution. Each function has had clearly identified tasks, and within these functional 'silos' or 'stovepipes' (as they have been called) there is a recognised hierarchy up which employees might hope to progress.

The problem with this approach is that it is inwardly focused and concentrates primarily upon the efficient use of resources rather than on the creation of outputs. The outputs of any business can only be measured in terms of customer satisfaction achieved at a profit. Paradoxically, these outputs can only be achieved by cross-functional co-ordination and co-operation across the organisation. These cross-functional linkages should follow the materials and information flows that connect the customer with the business and its suppliers. They are in fact the *core processes* of the business. In the responsive organisation the emphasis is upon the management of processes.

One of the thought leaders of process re-engineering, Thomas Davenport, has defined a process in an organisational context as:

> Any activity or group of activities that takes an input, adds value to it, and provides an output to an internal or external customer.

The characteristics of business processes include the following:

- They have customers for whom they create value
- They typically cross functional boundaries
- They draw upon functional resources
- They are team based
- They have strategic goals.

The challenge to the organisation is to break down the functional barriers to integration and instead become a market-facing business. The driving force for this change is the realisation that it is processes that create customer value, not functions. Therefore processes are the fundamental tasks that have to be achieved in order to create and deliver customer value.

In any business there are a number of core processes that should be managed on a cross-functional basis. Examples of core processes would include:

- Brand development (including new product development)
- Consumer development (primarily focused on building end-user loyalty)
- Customer management (creating relationships with inter-mediaries)
- Supplier development (strengthening upstream relationships)
- Supply chain management (including the order fulfilment process).

The shift from functional management to process management is summarised in Figure 6.1.

The transformation from a functional to a process-based organisation has major implications for the management structure of the business generally, and for marketing management in particular. In effect, in the process-based organisation marketing is no longer a series of activities performed within a marketing department. Indeed, in many companies that have made the transition from functions to processes the 'marketing department' has all but disappeared.

However, this is not to assume that marketing is dead; indeed the reverse is the case – the need for market-driven business is as strong now as it ever was. Rather, what we are seeing is the transformation of marketing from a narrow set of functional skills based upon a conventional '4 Ps' marketing mix to a broader business orientation where the delivery of superior customer value becomes the key objective. That said, it must be recognised that there are still important

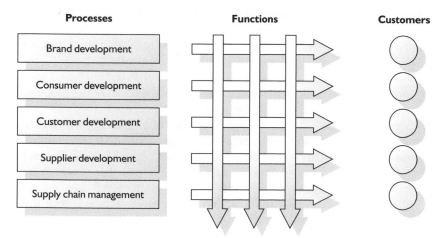

Figure 6.1 Managing cross-functional processes to create customer value

functional skills that marketing must continue to develop – for example, research to provide in-depth market understanding and knowledge of consumers' buying patterns, motivations and so forth.

Strategic marketing planning also takes on a different form in the process-based organisation. Essentially, the task of marketing planning in this new organisational model is to translate strategic goals into *process* plans. The principle is illustrated in the extended vignette later in this chapter, which describes how the brewer Guinness established the strategic goal of 'a perfect pint in every pub'. In that company the marketing planning task then became one of translating that goal into specific programmes for each process. So, for instance, what did 'a perfect pint in every pub' imply for the brand development process, the customer management process, and so on? With each process now managed by a cross-functional team, a wider, more integrated perspective is brought to bear upon the issue.

Some might argue that this underpinning integrative process of strategic marketing planning might better be termed strategic business planning. This is really only semantics, and in reality it does not matter what this critical process is called – only that we manage it and recognise its central importance.

The justification for this radically different view of the business is that these processes are in effect 'capabilities', and it is through capabilities that the organisation competes. In other words, the effectiveness of the new product development process, the order fulfilment process and so on determines the extent to which the business will succeed in the market place. Hence there is a need to manage capabilities and not just functions. Managing these underpinning 'core processes' to deliver customer value is key to market-place success.

In the process-orientated organisation, cross-functional teams are charged with achieving business goals defined in terms of customer value and customer profitability. This represents a radical shift from the traditional organisation that focused around functional management, and where the means of satisfying customer requirements was via a series of 'hand-offs' from one function to another.

Under this revised organisational model, the role of functional management is now quite different. Essentially it is to create 'pools of resource' or 'centres of excellence' from which process teams will draw their members. Unipart, a UK-based supplier of logistics services to the automotive, defence and healthcare sectors, has gone so far as to re-name its traditional functions as 'schools', the idea being that they should become centres of functional excellence, the major purpose of which is to provide training and development for process team members.

One of the most significant advantages of process teams is that they are customer facing and, as a result, tend to focus on ways in which opportunities can be created for further value enhancement. In particular, by focusing upon 'customer satisfaction' in its broadest

Managing cross-functional processes is becoming a critical source of competitive advantage

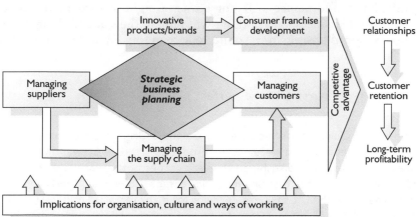

Supply chain processes aligned with customers' and suppliers' processes

Figure 6.2 Superior business processes

sense there is the inevitable recognition that marketing and logistics are irrevocably intertwined. Figure 6.2 suggests a revised organisational model that focuses upon the processes that directly or indirectly deliver customer satisfaction.

Businesses that wish to become market facing must by definition shift their orientation. They must find ways of managing across functions and co-ordinating all of the previously separate activities, from procurement through to distribution. Since customer satisfaction at a profit is the overriding aim of any commercial organisation, management of the 'customer satisfaction process' should be the priority.

Managing this radically different type of business needs a new set of skills and managerial capabilities. Interestingly, the emerging profession of logistics management is providing a key source of people capable of working in a cross-functional environment. By its very nature, logistics is an integrative, co-ordinating activity, and the managers who work in it tend to be well versed in the art of managing across functions. Logistics managers understand customer service, and they understand the trade-off opportunities in distribution. They also understand requirements planning and the need for procurement to be linked to the factory and beyond that to the warehouse. These same managers are accustomed to team-based working, and have facilitation and communication skills. In addition, they understand the opportunities that information technology can provide as the driving force for breaking down the functional barriers.

All this is not to suggest that the transition to a responsive process-based organisation will be straightforward. Organisational hierarchies have crumbled and layers of existing management may no longer be necessary; territories will be broken up; evaluating and rewarding individual performance will not be as straightforward in the new team-based business; and nothing will remain the same for long in an organisation that seeks to respond to a changing environment.

Guinness – in pursuit of the perfect pint

The brewer Guinness has been brewing Guinness Original stout since the end of the eighteenth century. Guinness's products, originally brewed in Dublin, are now brewed in or distributed to every corner of the globe, although the UK continues to be the brewer's single most important market. Beer consumption in the UK has been declining for many years, falling fastest in the traditional licensed trade sector (pubs and clubs). Unlike some other UK breweries, Guinness owns none of the licensed premises through which its products are sold; consequently it has no guaranteed outlets for its beers but has instead successfully relied on consumer demand to persuade customers and competitors to stock its products. Guinness stout held its ground well within this declining market, but in the early 1990s competition stiffened with the launch of a number of rival stouts and the rising popularity of imported bottled beers. Guinness had responded to changing market conditions with the introduction of new products and new advertising campaigns, but margins were under pressure as more and more consumers opted to buy beer for home consumption from their local supermarkets.

The prospect of intensified competition and the growing complexity of Guinness's product portfolio meant that costs had to be lowered and marketing effectiveness had to be improved to meet the rigours of the changing environment. The brewer was forced to re-examine the way it managed and organised its marketing activities within the organisation as a whole. 'Project Condor', a programme to improve the market-place focus of Guinness Brewing, was the result.

Project Condor aimed to engineer a shift away from Guinness's traditional functional focus towards a process orientation, reducing the number of 'functional fingers in the pie' – each of which built cost and delay into the operation. Improving quality and speed were therefore seen as integral objectives, and so was a substantial reduction in the number of staff in the brewing, marketing and administrative functions.

Marketing at Guinness had hitherto been organised on a product management basis, with separate sales and marketing functions. Under Project Condor, the old marketing and sales organisations were slimmed down and restructured around two new 'demand companies' – 'On Trade' and 'Off Trade' (serving supermarkets and other unlicensed channels) – plus a 'Consumer Marketing' group. The two 'demand companies' took over responsibility for sales and marketing management within their respective sectors, and for their customers' and their sectors' profitability. The new Consumer Marketing group handled brand management, and had wider corporate profitability responsibilities. Inevitably some overlapping and competing interests remained, but the reorganisation facilitated further efforts to improve performance on three strategic dimensions. The first was product leadership. Guinness believed that the future of its business was heavily dependent on product excellence, given that it owned none of its retail outlets. Second was customer intimacy, through greater concentration on the specific needs of distinct customer groups, and third was operational excellence, which would become even more critical with growing dependency on the low-return take-home business.

Project Condor put other changes in place within the business, not least the move from standard to Activity-Based Costing (ABC). Although hampered by the slow and expensive task of an IT upgrade, and the initial reluctance of the accounts department, the adoption of ABC quickly proved its worth. Investment decisions had always been made around the core brand, but it was anticipated that the peripheral brands could become more important if competition against Guinness Original stout continued to increase. Standard costing methods indicated that new brands were very profitable, but Guinness quickly discovered that previously hidden costs surfaced with the application of ABC. Under the new system, the set-up costs of a new brand were factored into the equation and so were the costs incurred through increased complexity. Suddenly the core brand, Guinness Original, appeared to be relatively more profitable than anyone had realised.

Guinness Original had always had a loyal following among older drinkers, and in the early 1990s an advertising campaign starring Rutger Hauer as the 'Man with the Guinness' had successfully positioned it as a quirky premium brand in the minds of younger drinkers. However, the 'pure genius' of the brand-building advertising could not turn curious or occasional drinkers into loyal customers. The product itself had to meet consumers' expectations if they were going to try it for a second time, and hopefully acquire a taste for the thick dark beer. Worryingly, though, it seemed that all too often the customer was presented with a less than perfect pint.

Guinness had just completed a £50 million brewery upgrade, and a quality audit established that the draught beer left the brewery in prime condition. Things were going awry somewhere downstream, but nobody knew exactly where. Remedying the problem fell beyond the remit of any single department at Guinness, so a cross-functional team was assembled to work on a solution. The rest of the product delivery process – from brewery to consumer – was studied, mapped and measured. The problems, it transpired, developed once the beer arrived at the licensed premises. Licensees did not always observe the brewer's recommendations for storage and presentation, and whilst both were beyond the direct control of Guinness, they were essential to the delivered quality of the product.

A plan was drawn up, outlining a programme that Guinness believed would, when implemented, consistently deliver 'the perfect pint'. Consideration was given to resourcing, training and communications, with key performance indicators identified and internal service levels agreements arranged at each step in the supply chain. The programme's progress was measured weekly, and its results communicated within Guinness's brewing division. Although Guinness had not purposefully developed cross-functional team working in the past, the foundations for such an approach had been laid two years earlier with 'Breakthrough'. Breakthrough was an internal marketing and communication programme that at the time aimed to align all employees behind the company's strategic objectives. The programme had a lasting effect, and the Internal Communications team established as part of the Breakthrough initiative became an important link in the Perfect Pint project.

To deliver the perfect pint, draught Guinness should be stored and served at a temperature of between 5 and 8°C, served in a straight 'Guinness' glass, and topped with a tight, creamy head 10–15 mm deep. To achieve the desired result the pint had to be dispensed in two parts, allowing most of the beer to settle for a minute before topping up the glass. Old established pubs already used the two-part pour, but other establishments needed a little more help. First, the actual pouring process was made easier by the development and installation of special founts, at a total cost of £70 000. A technical field team was created and dispatched, once the devices were installed, to train the licensees. After training the licensees received Perfect Pint training certificates, together with a range of two-part pour promotional material. These included instruction cards detailing the two-part pour technique, and Exchange Cards that, after a number of recorded purchases, could be redeemed by the consumer in exchange for Guinness merchandise (T-shirts, lapel pins etc.). A television advertising campaign was commissioned to support the initiative, a version of which was also released on the Internet and quickly became a cult screensaver.

Guinness Original stout went on to achieve its highest ever share of the total draft beer market. The process management approach used to deliver the perfect pint was so successful that Guinness has used cross-functional teams to identify and streamline other key business processes, including order handling (order to cash), new product and packaging development, and category management.

From products to customers

Even though the marketing concept – a customer and market orientation – has gained widespread acceptance across industry, there is still an underlying tendency to manage products rather than customers. This emphasis is reflected in job titles such as 'brand manager' and 'product group manager', and in accounting systems that can provide precise information on product profitability but are incapable of measuring the profitability of customers.

Customer satisfaction at a profit has to be the ultimate objective of any commercial organisation, and hence it is imperative that the management structures and the measurement systems also mirror this. In organisational terms the requirement is to create a means whereby markets, channels and customers can be managed, and appropriate accounting and control procedures can be implemented.

Market-facing 'demand management' has emerged in companies like Guinness as an integrating, cross-functional approach to servicing customers. As suggested in Chapter 3, this transformation requires a greater emphasis on 'customer value' and not just 'brand value'. Essentially, this means that the supplying organisation must focus its efforts upon developing an 'offer' or 'package' that will positively impact customers' perceptions of the value that they derive through ownership of that offer. The argument that is increasingly being voiced is that a critical component of such customer value is service. In a sense we are approaching the time when logistics and marketing need to be managed conjointly.

Traditionally, the major focus of marketing has – at least in consumer markets – been upon the end-user and upon the development of brand loyalty. However, of late there has been a growing recognition of the importance of building relationships with marketing and distribution intermediaries, who often control the access to the end-user or consumer. These intermediaries could be retailers, distributors, stockists or wholesalers, or indeed original equipment manufacturers (OEMs). Without their support and co-operation it is becoming more and more difficult to achieve success in the final market place. As a result, many companies are refocusing their marketing strategies to place a greater emphasis upon the development and management of customer relationships.

To a certain extent the shift in the balance of power away from the supplier to the customer is forcing a reappraisal of traditional trading arrangements. Even allowing for this, however, there are strong arguments from the standpoint of competitive advantage for seeking closer relationships with customers. One of the key reasons for wishing to achieve 'preferred supplier' status is the obvious one – that it provides a strong barrier to entry to potential competitors. For instance, in the first year that Procter & Gamble forged a supply chain relationship with Wal-Mart in the USA, they increased their sales through that outlet by 40 per cent. Much of the additional shelf space they gained came from competitive brands. The move allowed P&G to take a much more active role in demand management – in that instance in the form of category management.

Category management

ECR Europe defines category management as: 'the strategic management of product categories to maximise profit and satisfy consumer

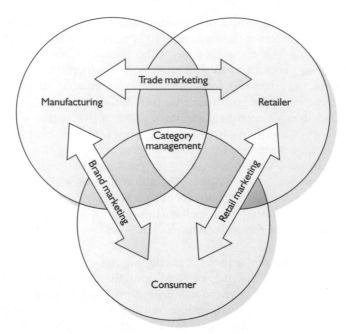

Figure 6.3 Category management (*Source*: **Adapted from Glendinning Management Consultants' Intergrowth**[TM] **Model)**

needs'. Category management predates ECR, and is itself maturing as a concept as practitioners and researchers gradually gain better insights into the role it can play in generating more business. So far in this book we have tended to address category management simply from an efficiency or productivity perspective, but maximising the efficiency of category management is only half of the story. Effective collaboration on category management should pool and leverage the knowledge of retailer and suppliers to lead to better collective demand management and a more attractive offer for the consumer. Figure 6.3 illustrates the category management concept, presenting it as a fusion of brand, trade and retail marketing.

In practice, category management has frequently failed to integrate these three important elements. Part of the problem is that it has often been presented primarily as an operations efficiency meets trade marketing issue, requiring the appointment of a sophisticated branded goods supplier to manage retailers' shelf space on their behalf. The supplier would assume responsibility for ranging and assortment within its own category, which would enable it to improve its operating efficiency and the retailers' return on shelf space – thus maximising retailer profits for both parties. This is fine as far as it goes, but only really addresses the concerns of the retailer–manufacturer/ buyer–seller interface, as illustrated in Figure 6.4(a). It overlooks the

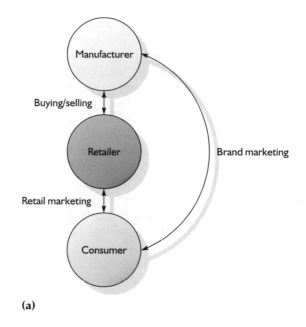

(a)

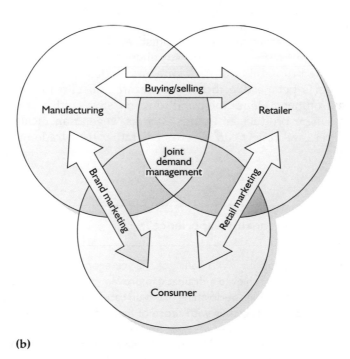

(b)

Figure 6.4 (a) Traditional interface; (b) Demand management interface (*Source*: Adapted from Glendinning Management Consultants' Inter-growth™ Model)

wider needs of the other vital group of interested parties – the end customers or consumers.

It can of course be argued that branded goods suppliers bring with them decades of expertise in consumer marketing and brand management. In practice, though, some retailers have found that passing too much responsibility over to a single leading supplier can result in 'efficient' but unimaginative solutions. The notion that category management can be best effected by collaboration between a retailer and a single supplier acting as 'category captain' is therefore being reappraised. Over-reliance on the category captain can also encourage a tendency to view each product category as a stand-alone profit centre, whereas in reality the management of one category cannot be divorced from complementary categories. Furthermore, it can lead to a situation where within-category management is out of step with the retailer's wider strategic marketing objectives.

The need to align category management with retail marketing objectives has prompted some to explore better and more comprehensive approaches to joint demand management. Furthermore, the retailer is likely to have considerable knowledge of its own customer base, which, if shared with a leading supplier, should in theory lead to a more effective approach. Figure 6.4(b) depicts the emerging shape of demand management interfaces.

In the UK the larger and more sophisticated retailers are becoming adept at co-ordinating primary suppliers, having recognised that although the profitability of each category is clearly important, from the shopper's perspective the categories are still part of the overall retail environment. Hence the trend towards 'store-within-store' retail formats, where product groupings such as 'vegetarian meals', 'baby care' or 'pet care' reflect consumer needs rather than trade marketing agendas.

From category to 'beauty experience'

ASDA/Wal-Mart, working with one of its category captains, make-up manufacturer L'Oréal, achieved a dramatic improvement in sales by redefining the objectives for its under-performing make-up category. It did so by bringing several L'Oréal brands together with those of head-to-head competitors in a single aisle format to create a more interesting and enjoyable 'beauty experience' for the customers. The new 'store-within-store' format resulted in a 21 per cent increase in sales of make-up and a 27 per cent overall increase in toiletries sales, much of this due to higher impulse purchasing of complementary products.

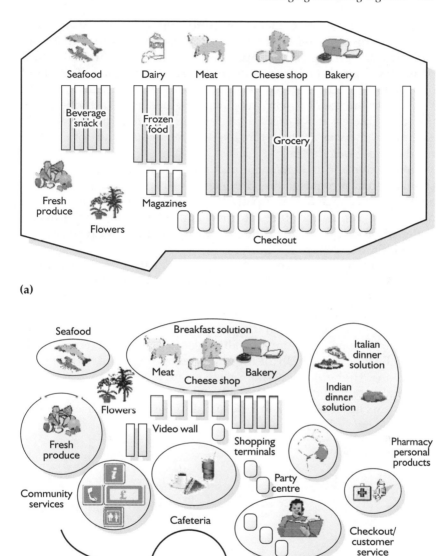

Figure 6.5 (a) Traditional store layout; (b) Future store layout

Aisle management can, if successfully implemented, effect a strategic repositioning of the category and the store as a 'destination' – i.e. somewhere so attractive to consumers that they will make it their preferred shopping location. Figure 6.5 illustrates how changing approaches to demand management are reshaping store layouts.

Back at the product level, category managers and logisticians must still deal with the vagaries of tactical promotions. One option, of course, would be for retailers simply to follow the P&G/Wal-Mart example – dispense with tactical promotions and opt instead for an everyday low-pricing value proposition. However, with around a third of all FMCG goods in Europe sold under trade promotion of one kind or another, few European retailers have been willing to abandon them. Promotions are seen by many retailers as value-adding activities; they introduce interest and variety to the consumers' shopping experience. Tactical promotions are therefore likely to remain a feature of retailing for the foreseeable future.

From a demand management and replenishment point of view, it should also be recognised that the extent to which tactical promotional activity will change demand patterns is linked to the role the item in question plays within the category and wider store assortment. Different products perform different roles within the category or aisle, and within the store as a whole.

One approach to segmentation used in category management classifies products into the four roles shown in the two-by-two matrix in Figure 6.6. The two dimensions used to create the matrix are frequency of purchase (high *vs* low number of times purchased per year), and household penetration (high *vs* low percentage of house-holds purchasing). Terminology diverges here, with different labels used in Europe and the US for the four category roles, but the principle is the same. High-frequency, high-penetration products, such as coffee, milk and breakfast cereals, are referred to as 'staples' or 'destination' categories. High-frequency, low-penetration products, such as yogurts,

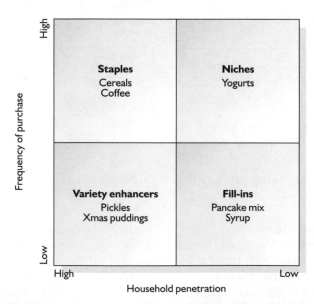

Figure 6.6 Category roles (*Source*: Based on Hoch, S. J. and Pomerantz, John J. (2002) How effective is category management? *ECR Journal*, **2(1), 26–32)**

are 'niches' or 'preferred'. Low-frequency, high-penetration products are the 'seasonal/occasional' purchases or 'variety enhancers', and include items like pickles and Christmas puddings. The low-frequency, low-penetration quadrant consists of the 'fill-ins' or 'convenience' products, such as baking mixes or syrups.

Categories and promotional response

Research by Hoch and Pomerantz examined the performance of 19 food product categories in 106 major supermarket chains operating in the USA. Their research gave manufacturers and retailers an insight into how tactical marketing resources could be used to best effect, by identifying the likely impact of various promotional activities or merchandising decisions on the different category types.

For example, price sensitivity and promotional responsiveness is in fact highest in categories where customers purchase frequently – i.e. for staples and, to a lesser extent, the variety enhancing/seasonal categories.

High-frequency purchases shape customers' perceptions of store prices in general, and hence their influence on the consumers' choice of destination. Most retailers are therefore keen to keep prices in staple/destination categories low for fear of harming store traffic. This has had a tendency to lower margins across the sector, limiting the retailers' scope for generating high returns by reducing everyday prices for these product categories – unless, that is, they are accompanied by significant cost savings. It could be argued that reducing everyday prices is more likely to realise performance improvements in variety enhancing/occasional/seasonal and in niche/preferred categories. However, Hoch and Pomerantz suggest that in practice these categories may not be price-elastic enough to justify everyday low prices.

Temporary price reductions were found to have a significant impact on demand for high-traffic staples, but little effect on niche/preferred products. In-store promotions offering temporary price reductions impact demand for frequently visited categories by encouraging opportunistic purchases, but do nothing to build overall volume of store traffic. Furthermore, in-store promotions discounting low-traffic fill-in/convenience categories would have little impact because few customers visit these categories in the first place.

The impact of external advertising has been found to have the greatest impact on staples/destination categories, it will have some impact on demand for niche/preferred and occasional or seasonal/variety enhancers, but little on the fill-in/convenience products. However, in-store displays are likely to be effective for fill-ins because they draw customers' attention to the category, mainly because ancillary off-shelf displays dramatically increase the shelf space and exposure relative to their usual shelf set.

When it came to matters of assortment, Hoch and Pomerantz found that increased breadth (number of brands) and depth of assortment (number of

SKUs) had a positive effect on most categories and in building store traffic, because greater variety meant that retailers could better cater for the heterogeneous tastes of their customers. The only exception was with staples/destination categories. Product proliferation and brand extensions meant that staple categories were likely to be close to saturation already, and that further investment in this area would lead to diminishing returns. Efforts by FMCG manufacturers to reduce the number of brands and SKUs in saturated staple categories were likely to improve efficiency and, provided the deleted lines were not favourites, were unlikely to affect customers' intentions to purchase at a store.

(Source: Based on material from Hoch, S. J. and Pomerantz, John J. (2002) How effective is category management? *ECR Journal*, **2(1)**, 26–32.)

All of the above should serve to illustrate that category management as a process is time-consuming and complex. IT solutions are available to assist but, like many of those on offer for CPFR, they are far from perfect and some can be dangerously rigid in the face of on-coming flexible web-services. For all the difficulties, though, category management has the potential to lead to the Holy Grail of retail management – significant increases in sales, optimised assortment and inventory, and increased consumer satisfaction.

Outside of the retail environment, similar opportunities exist for enhancing customer value. 'Key Account Management' is increasingly replacing classic sales management as customers grow in size and in purchasing power. The issue, as in retailing, is to find ways in which the supplying company can enhance the profitability of its customers' business. In other words, rather than focus on selling products to customers, focus instead on creating value for them. For example, in the offshore oil exploration and production business it is now not unusual to find suppliers to the exploration and production companies providing a range of value-adding services on a 'one-stop' shopping basis. So, for instance, a large integrated supplier such as Kellogg Brown and Root or Foster Wheeler will manage the inventories of spares and consumables for customers such as ConocoPhillips or ChevronTexaco on the basis of shared information on usage.

Key account management should also be team based and cross functional if it is to facilitate the search for opportunities to create customer value. In the consumer goods sector, companies such as Kraft and Procter & Gamble have replaced product-based divisional sales forces with cross-functional teams to relate to major accounts.

Figure 6.7 shows how at Kraft customer teams are supported by category teams and process teams so that an integrated business-wide approach may be adopted for all major accounts.

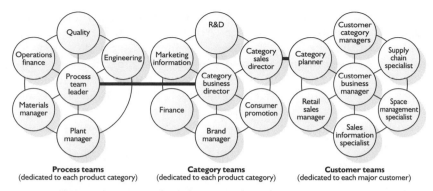

Process teams
(dedicated to each product category)

Category teams
(dedicated to each product category)

Customer teams
(dedicated to each major customer)

Figure 6.7 **Managing through teams at Kraft (***Source***: George, M., Freeling, A. and Court, D. (1994) Reinventing the marketing organisation,** *McKinsey Quarterly,* **No. 4. Copyright 1994 McKinsey & Company. All rights reserved)**

From profit to performance

Whilst there can be no argument that long-term, sustained profit has to be the goal of any commercial organisation, there is a growing realisation that if profit is the *end*, then we should spend more time examining the *means* whereby it is achieved. So many management boards begin their weekly meetings with a review of the financial position – in other words, before anything else is discussed revenues will be examined and costs detailed at some length. Ratios, production efficiencies – these are the currency by which the business is measured and therefore controlled. These conventional measures have tended to monitor functional performance and to be focused upon efficiency. Process-orientated measures, on the other hand, emphasise such things as customer satisfaction, throughput times and cost-to-serve.

Conventional cost accounting systems reflect the functional/effi-ciency bias, and were originally geared to the requirements of mass-production manufacturing. They incorporated assumptions of stable and predictable markets, long product life cycles and large production runs, with a generous proportion of direct variable costs incorporated into total product costs.

Logistics activities were simply not high enough up the managerial agenda to warrant significant attention in the organisations for which conventional cost accounting systems were designed to serve. The emphasis was on the need to understand product costs, not the costs associated with servicing particular customers.

Today it is clear that the assumptions underpinning traditional cost accounting methods no longer hold true for an increasing proportion of organisations. The methods themselves have been shown to be inappropriate and incomplete ways of assessing performance in a process-driven, market-orientated organisation. Instead companies are turning to activity-based costing (ABC) and throughput costing to understand the true costs of processes, which can provide a basis for establishing performance indicators in marketing logistics.

ABC focuses on the identification of cost drivers so that costs can be attributed directly to the activities that create them. In doing so, it links costs to processes instead of attributing them to individual units on an almost arbitrary basis. By focusing on activities it allows differences in ordering behaviour, distribution, product mix requirements and merchandising support to be identified, as well as the costs of invoicing and collection. Throughput costing is the end-to-end application of ABC; it calculates the total cost along an entire process. The result is a clearer picture of the true 'cost-to-serve', and hence the profitability of customers. Its use makes it possible to identify the aspects of service that create cost and, where necessary, to modify the service package on a customer-by-customer basis. It can also focus attention upon ways in which the order fulfilment process can be amended to improve overall Economic Value Added (EVA).

EVA is a relatively simple but useful financial performance measure. It is the difference between the company's net operating profit after taxes and the cost of capital. If the difference is positive, the company is creating wealth for its shareholders; if negative, it is destroying wealth! Whilst it is a simple concept, it is not always fully understand. Sometimes the true cost of capital is underestimated. Properly speaking, the cost of capital to an organisation is the weighted average cost of its debt and its equity. The cost of its debt is easy to identify, but the cost of equity is more debatable. The appropriate cost concept to use here is 'opportunity cost' – the return a shareholder could expect to get elsewhere – with some adjustment for the 'riskiness' of the business.

The definition of capital employed should also be broadened to include R&D, intellectual capital and brand building activity.

Once the concept of EVA is accepted and understood within the organisation, it can then be applied to the various activities of the business – for example, serving different markets or distribution channels. It is particularly helpful in measuring logistics performance. Shortening end-to-end pipeline time can, for instance, significantly improve EVA by reducing the inventory in the pipeline whilst simultaneously reducing costs. Similarly, programmes that focus on improving 'perfect order' achievement build EVA by minimising invoice queries and adjustments, and hence reducing accounts receivable.

There is a saying that 'what gets measured gets managed', implying that the choice of performance measure determines behaviour. Thus whatever tools and techniques may be used, the fundamental question is: are we measuring the right things and using the appropriate metrics? For example, in a business where employees are required to 'clock' in and out of work each day, punctuality may be improved but their willingness to work more than the agreed hours may be reduced. Hence the importance of understanding what the critical performance criteria are, and therefore what we should be measuring. The underlying logic of this viewpoint is that performance drives profitability – if we get the right performance, then profit will follow.

One approach to measuring, monitoring and improving process performance is *benchmarking*. By examining in detail how other organisations create value for their customers and how they manage the value-creation processes, we can learn a great deal about our own processes and their effectiveness when measured against appropriate key performance indicators (KPIs).

'Best of class' benchmarking

Benchmarking is a continuous improvement technique that considers how well an organisation performs against key performance indicators. The technique can be used to assess individual products, services, skills, management practices or processes. Its principle advantage is that it looks beyond existing internally defined standards by examining performance relative to 'best of breed' competitors and, for maximum effect, to 'best of class' alternatives drawn from other industries.

The office equipment company Xerox is one of the best-known exponents of benchmarking. It took up competitive benchmarking in the 1980s out of defensive necessity when Japanese photocopier manufacturer Canon began making very significant inroads into Xerox's major markets. Xerox began with product benchmarking, mostly reverse engineering competitor's equipment, but soon realised that this only allowed it to understand how far behind its products had fallen. The company recognised that comparisons to 'best of breed' finished products were the result of superior new product design and supplier management processes. To outperform its competitors, Xerox decided that it would have to benchmark not just against 'best of breed' but also against 'best of class' practices and processes drawn from other sectors of industry.

Benchmarking against 'best of class' offers several advantages over and above competitor comparisons. First, it bypasses the sensitivities of dealing with direct competitors. It facilitates open discussions between representatives of different firms as well as the exchanges of KPI data and site visits between co-operating parties – all are necessary parts of the benchmarking process.

The second big advantage in looking beyond the confines of your organisation's own industry is that it is possible to identify ways to leapfrog current 'best of breed' competitors. It can also provide forewarning of the effects of impending technological advances – advances that may have already impacted practices in other industries, but have not yet reached other sectors.

Third, because benchmarking properly performed reveals inefficiencies in well-established processes, questions will be raised about how current processes are structured and managed. Personnel have been found to be much more willing to adopt new 'best practice' solutions adapted from other industries then they are when presented with new ways of working that have been borrowed directly from their competitors. The task of importing and adapting approaches new to the industry to provide truly innovative solutions is a morale lifting and creative process. It requires the involvement of line personnel as well as management.

In a process-orientated company, many of these new performance indicators used in benchmarking and elsewhere are non-financial. That is, they will focus management's attention upon the truly critical areas of performance – i.e. those that drive profitability and align the business unit with its strategic goals. In the case of marketing logistics, we might expect to see metrics that capture such things as customer satisfaction, flexibility and employee commitment. Management meetings should therefore begin their agenda not with the financial review – that will come later – but with a review of non-financial performance indicators. These will necessarily differ between organisations, but may include:

1 Customer satisfaction
   - Customer retention
   - Brand preference
   - Dealer satisfaction
   - Service performance
2 Flexibility
   - Set-up times
   - Commonality of components and materials
   - Throughput times
   - Percentage value-added time
3 People commitment
   - Employee turnover
   - Suggestions submitted and implemented
   - Internal service climate and culture
   - Training and development index.

The whole notion of adopting broad-based performance measurement systems was brought to the fore by writers Kaplan and Norton, who popularised the concept of a 'Balanced Scorecard' for measuring business unit performance (Kaplan, R. S. and Norton, D. P. (1992) The balanced scorecard: measures that drive performance, *Harvard Business Review*, Jan./Feb., pp 71–9). Their scorecard used multiple measures from four perspectives – financial, customer, internal business processes, and learning and growth – to provide a balanced picture of current operating performance as well as the drivers of future performance. Well-worn financial measures (such as inventory turns or day's sales outstanding) are single-firm, internally focused indications of past performance, whereas well-chosen non-financial measures can be forward and outward looking. They indicate forthcoming performance and future direction, and incorporate external perspectives – not least those of customers – into the system.

The balanced scorecard approach, although designed to provide a performance measurement system for single business units, has since been embraced as a model for the implementation of much more ambitious supply chain integration programmes. The ECR scorecard shown in Figure 6.8 is one such example. The ECR scorecard was devised as an enabling tool, to provide companies in all parts of the supply chain and of any size with a means of answering 'how well are we doing?'. Its creators were at pains to point out that it offered a point of reference; it would not generate business or customer and supply chain improvements on its own. It would, however, identify areas for potential improvement both internally and externally – i.e. between trading partners.

The scorecard covers demand and supply side implementation measures, and it promotes the use of ABC as an appropriate cost accounting system.

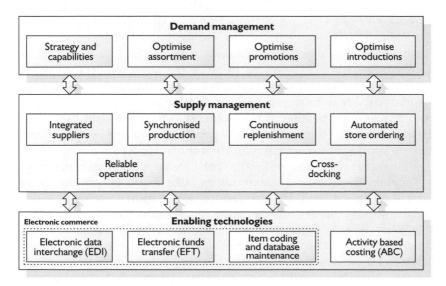

Figure 6.8 ECR scorecard (*Source*: ECR Europe)

ABC accounting and aspects of demand management have already been covered elsewhere in this chapter, and aspects of product supply and replenishment were covered in previous ones. There are, however, other aspects of supplier management, such as supplier selection and development, that we have not yet visited. In an integrated supply chain context they warrant managerial attention.

Just as businesses have become more adept at setting internal or customer-focused performance improvement measures, the larger and more influential ones have also become more actively involved in applying the same tools and techniques to monitor the performance of their suppliers.

The concept of *supplier development* proposes that it is in the best interests of the customer to take a proactive approach to the establishment of mutually beneficial – though not necessarily equitable – relationships with suppliers. In other words, customers should actively seek ways in which they can work together with suppliers to reduce the total costs of ownership. They should do so whilst constantly seeking to enhance their own differentiation through means such as improved quality, innovative design and unique technologies, all of which will be strongly influenced by supplier involvement.

Supplier development programmes, largely based on the Toyota Production System, are commonplace in the car industry, where the notion of managing a cohort of first-tier suppliers as an extension of the manufacturer's enterprise is widely accepted. The 'extended enterprise' model has since been adopted in other manufacturing sectors with high engineering content, such as aerospace. Versions of the extended enterprise can also be found in the apparel industry, where companies like Benetton and Marks & Spencer have historically maintained close working relationships with dedicated suppliers. The model has also made the transition into food and grocery retailing, as is shown by the Gunstones Bakery example in Chapter 2. Here demanding customers – in this instance the large retailers – look to preferred suppliers to align with their processes while undertaking rigorous quality improvement and cost-reduction programmes. In this way a 'seamless' pipeline can be created, which not only makes for greater efficiency through reduced paperwork, lower inventory and faster response, but also creates an environment in which the search for continual cost reduction and value enhancement becomes a priority.

Supplier development programmes, like most other aspects of supply chain integration programmes, are resource intensive. Such collaborations demand close working relationships with a few leading suppliers, whose ongoing performance is carefully monitored and benchmarked according to appropriate KPIs. The KPIs will vary between businesses and industries, but are likely to include aspects of quality, cost and delivery, as well as partnership management criteria.

A willingness on both sides to work co-operatively for long-term mutual gain is a prerequisite for any supplier management programme. The likelihood is that establishing such programmes for the first time will require a fundamental shift in attitudes on both sides. This should not be taken to mean that partnership working implies a weakening in the desire to improve performance – indeed, successful partnerships in the supply chain tend to be based very much on hard commercial realities. When they become commercially unviable, possibly as a result of changes in the market place or the competitive environment, the likelihood is that they will be dissolved. This is a theme that will be revisited in Chapter 7, when we deal with the issues of globalisation and how that affects the management of marketing logistics.

Managing marketing logistics: key issues

- The need for organisational change
  - From functions to processes
  - From products to customers
  - From profit to performance

- Manage processes, not just functions
  - Processes are competitive capabilities
  - Processes require functional excellence to support them
  - Processes create customer value

- Manage supply and demand, not just products
  - Bridging the gap between manufacturer and retailer
  - Sharing knowledge through joint category planning
  - Understanding consumer response to promotions

- What gets measured gets managed
  - The importance of performance measurement
  - Use non-financial performance indicators
  - Focus on internal and external customer satisfaction

Chapter 7

Serving the global customer

One of the most striking trends in recent years has been the globalisation of markets, organisations and industries. Its impact can not only be seen through the global reach of well-established brands like Coca-Cola, Marlboro or Gucci, but it is also apparent in markets as diverse as computing, automobiles and consumer electronics. Nor is the trend towards globalisation confined only to products; we see similar transformations in services such as banking, retailing and satellite TV.

The corporations that have created and developed these global brands are expanding and refocusing their operations so that they too are global in scope. What this means is that an electronics company, for example, may source some of its components in one country and sub-assemble in another, with final assembly taking place in a third country.

The motivation for this is largely economic, based upon the search for cost reduction. The cost savings may be available through lower labour rates, lower costs of material, lower taxes, lower costs of capital, or greater government assistance. At the same time, these organisations may also rationalise production so that individual country operations no longer produce a full range of products for their own national markets. Instead the company may focus production on fewer factories making a limited range of items, but for a regional or even global market. These strategies yield savings in manufacturing costs, but the logistical challenges they present are significant.

Not so many decades ago vertically integrated businesses were the norm, with large corporations active in every stage of the value creation and delivery process. Corporations like Ford and Courtaulds typified this approach. Ford owned everything from sources of raw materials (including steel mills and rubber plantations) right through to the final assembly of its motorcars. Courtaulds' reach extended from fibre manufacturing to branded consumer goods. Whilst some companies undoubtedly benefited from control of the sources of materials or guaranteed routes to market, these corporations fared badly in the face of rapid technological change, the deregulation of markets and the on-rush of intensified global competition. These forces continue to alter the dynamics of the market place, changing the basis of competition with the ensuing shifts in channel power.

As seen in earlier chapters, competitive pressures have encouraged organisations to re-examine their value chains, reducing costs and improving quality at every stage. They have retained 'core competencies', and outsourced almost everything else to specialist, preferably lower-cost, suppliers.

This latter model required a different sort of integration with suppliers of these outsourced activities. Instead of integration of ownership and control, it is an integration that is likely to be based upon the sharing of information and the creation of compatible strategic goals. This is the concept of 'virtual' integration. These organisations have moved along an evolutionary continuum towards a type of network structure, thought by many to be the most appropriate way of balancing the competing demands of greater organisational specialisation and flexibility.

Commentators have also suggested that as global brands continue to develop and industries seek ever-greater economies of scale, the need to implement transnational business strategies has become ever more pressing. Some organisations have gone further still, turning to partnerships and strategic alliances with customers and competitors to expand their global reach. Manufacturers such as Unilever, Nestlé and Danone have actively sought to strengthen their presence in world markets through carefully targeted acquisitions. At the same time they have attempted to improve their focus by disposing of brands that they see as marginal to their mainstream strategy.

The steady removal of trade barriers has revealed overcapacity in many sectors, and so concurrent with organisational change is the reshaping of operations and the rationalisation of production facilities. Unilever, for example, has formed two global divisions: one focused on food and the other on home and personal care. It has chosen to reduce its manufacturing sites around the globe from around 400 to under 300.

Retailers have followed the same trend to globalisation. In some cases this has been by organic growth, in others through acquisition. In recent years the UK-based Tesco has built its position in Central Europe and in the Far East, first through joint ventures and then through acquisition. Meanwhile, Wal-Mart has extended its presence in Germany, the UK and Japan through acquisition. Royal Ahold, from the Netherlands, has expanded around the world in the same way.

As retailers become global, they are moving their sourcing strategy in the same direction. Central buying from global sources is one way in which they can leverage their significant buying power.

The global business is therefore distinguished not only by its search for wider markets, but also by the tendency to source its materials and components on a worldwide basis and to manufacture in whatever locations provide optimum costs.

The logic of the global corporation is clear: it seeks to grow its business by extending its markets; at the same time it aims to achieve consistency in marketing and product ranges whilst achieving cost reduction through scale economies in purchasing and production (through focused manufacturing and/or assembly operations) and in logistics.

However, whilst the logic of globalisation is strong, we must recognise that it also presents certain challenges. First, world markets are still not homogenous; there remains a requirement for local variation in many product categories. Secondly, unless there is a high level of co-ordination the complex logistics of managing global supply chains may result in higher costs.

These two challenges are related: on the one hand, how to offer local markets the variety they seek whilst still gaining the advantage of standardised global production, and on the other, how to manage the links in the global chain from sources of supply through to end-user. There is a danger that as they globalise, companies may take too narrow a view of cost and only see the cost reduction that may be achieved by focusing production. In reality it is a total cost trade-off, where the costs of longer supply pipelines may sometimes outweigh the production cost saving.

Many other issues are raised by the spread of globalisation. Concerns have been expressed about the impact of the growth of outsourcing, leading to the emergence of the 'hollow corporation', and about the trend to offshore manufacturing, with the consequent implications for employment and the environment.

Further questions arise concerning the apparent contradiction between the move to globalisation – with the potential increase in lead times – and the search for just-in-time, zero inventory type strategies, which require shorter, not longer, pipelines. These are themes to which we will return at the end of this chapter.

Developing a global logistics strategy

A number of issues arise when global logistics strategies are being considered. One key concern is the question of the appropriate degree of centralised direction as against local autonomy. Traditionally many companies have preferred to devolve decision-making to a local level, yet almost by definition it is difficult to see how global supply chains can be optimised in terms of service and cost if they are planned and managed on a fragmented, local basis. On the other hand the attractions of local autonomy are clear, in terms of responsiveness to the market and the ability to 'stay close to the customer'.

A second, related issue is the extent to which synergy can be released by global co-ordination, and whether this is compatible with local decision-making in sourcing, production and distribution. Many global companies, for example, have sought to establish 'centres of excellence', particularly in R&D and in production, whereby resources and/or technologies are concentrated for greater focus. However, separating new product development and production from the market may not necessarily be sound practice, especially where those markets are not homogenous.

Running in parallel with these two issues is the question of how the search for economies of scale in production and the benefits of standardisation can be reconciled with the need to meet different local requirements and to do so with ever-higher levels of responsiveness.

Each of these three issues has significant implications for the way in which logistics is positioned organisationally in the global business, and each is examined in detail below.

Centralisation *vs* local autonomy

There is a widely held view that globalisation implies centralisation of management and control. However, whilst there are attractions to central planning and strategy formulation, there is a basic conflict with the ever-present need to stay as close to local markets as possible.

In the case of logistics planning, the need for central decision-making but with local implementation is strong. Many companies have gone beyond the centralisation of decision-making to centralise production and distribution facilities. The concept of the 'focused factory' has taken hold in Europe, spurred on in the 1990s by political changes and further development of the European Single Market. Focused factories, as the name implies, concentrate on the production of a limited range of products often sharing a similar manufacturing process or technology. So whereas in the past companies might have factories in individual countries producing the full range of products for that country, now they might have fewer locations with each factory specialising in a unique product portfolio but producing goods in greater volumes.

An inevitable effect of focused factories is the greater complexity of transport and distribution, as one factory now serves multinational markets. Also, whilst substantial opportunities for economies of scale through centralised production may exist in many industries, there may also be the risk of longer lead times and the loss of flexibility in meeting local customer needs. Because local tastes can still be quite different, it is essential that the global business does not confuse the need for centralised strategy determination and pipeline co-ordination with the overly simplistic idea that globalisation is only about economies of scale in production.

In fact, many organisations are now learning that it is possible to co-ordinate logistics centrally and yet meet local needs cost-effectively. This is achieved by linking individual facilities, sales offices and supply sources through shared information. The concept now is one of 'distributed distribution'. What this in effect means is that we manage production and inventory as if they were centralised, but the actual physical location of production and inventories is determined by other factors – specifically, the market and/or sources of supply. The idea of 'virtual' inventory is central to this approach. Virtual inventory is managed as if it were a single inventory – allowing the total inventory in the system to be substantially reduced – yet it may be physically dispersed according to where it is most appropriate to hold it. SKF, through its Global Forecasting and Supply System (GFSS), is able to manage demand across Europe through a single centre, allocate production to specific plants, schedule transport between plants and local trans-shipment points and, in so doing, dramatically improve customer service but with much reduced total inventory and better utilisation of production capacity.

Virtual inventory and the square root rule

It has long been recognised that by reducing the number of stock locations and consolidating inventory in fewer places, higher levels of service can be achieved with less total inventory.

This benefit is achieved through what might be termed 'risk pooling', so that demand variability in more than one market is covered by the same safety stock. The rule of thumb that generally applies in determining the reduction in total system inventory following a rationalisation in the number of locations is called the 'square root rule', which tells us that the reduction in inventory will be proportionate to the square root of the number of stock locations before and after the rationalisation. Hence a reduction in worldwide stock locations from, say, 100 to 25 would lead to a reduction in inventory of approximately 50 per cent, i.e. in the ratio of $\sqrt{100}:\sqrt{25}$, or 10:5.

Interestingly, it is not actually necessary *physically* to reduce the number of stock locations to achieve the benefits of the square root rule. All that is required is that the inventory be managed as if it were one inventory – in other words, to control it centrally. The idea behind *virtual inventory* is that the computer becomes the warehouse, and that stock levels are determined centrally on the basis of total visibility of demand from all sources. The location of specific stock will be determined according to where it makes greatest sense to keep it.

It must also be recognised that whilst the inventory savings can be substantial through virtual inventory the costs of transport will usually be higher, as product is moved greater distances in smaller quantities.

Achieving global synergies

The concept of synergy is simple: the whole should be more than the sum of the parts. It is often described as the '2 + 2 = 5' effect. The search for synergy is one of the main drivers of the trend towards the globalisation of industry, particularly in manufacturing and logistics.

It has often been suggested that there can be significant benefits if R&D, product development, manufacturing and marketing can be co-ordinated in order to avoid 're-inventing the wheel' country by country, and also through economies of scale in procurement and production.

Japanese companies have approached world markets in a noticeably co-ordinated way in industries such as automobiles, consumer electronics and machine tools. Even where they have established offshore manufacturing in the form of European 'transplant' factories, they still seek to ensure that they are managed within the framework of their worldwide strategy.

In areas such as procurement, opportunities exist for significant economies through centralised purchasing. Many multinational companies (i.e. companies with multiple local operations) found that they were incurring considerable cost penalties by sourcing components, packaging material, transport and other services locally and independently.

Perhaps the biggest opportunity for global synergy lies in the co-ordination of the physical logistics system. If companies are organised nationally with a high level of local autonomy in logistics management, then the likelihood is that there will be a cost penalty that can significantly erode profits. Hence the pressure that now exists in such companies to centralise the co-ordination of transportation and warehousing, and to balance worldwide flows of product and inventory decisions.

A key area for the achievement of global synergy is through the use of global order management and information systems. With complete visibility of worldwide demand and supply, the organisation can identify least-cost service options – for example, which customers should be sourced from which location so as to achieve optimum production and transportation economies whilst minimising inventory. Communications technology enables organisations, if they wish, to centralise order management and customer service through call centres, where the customer only places a local call. Whilst many companies prefer to localise their customer liaison through, for example, local sales offices, there is no reason why at the same time order processing and management cannot be centralised.

Standardised yet customised

Much has been written about the globalisation of markets, but we must be careful not to assume that the world is necessarily ready for standard products. There are still considerable differences in local tastes, preferences and requirements. For example, language differences mean that packaging will often need to be specific to a country or region, and local regulations may require product modification and so on.

All of this presents a significant challenge to the management of the global logistics system. For example, even a basic personal computer will need to be produced in different versions to take account of local voltage and plug type, and the keyboard and manuals will need to take account of the language of the user, as might the software itself.

A number of issues are raised by the need to 'localise' products, particularly in a production-orientated environment where the goal is more normally to seek unit cost reduction by producing a uniform product in volume. Specifically, the questions to be answered are:

- Can the final configuration or assembly of the product be delayed until real demand is ascertained?
- At what level in the chain should inventory be held, and where should final configuration take place?
- Where should the forecast be made – in the local market, or at the centre?

The first issue concerns 'postponement', an idea dealt with in Chapter 5. The benefits of postponement are reduced inventory holdings and greater overall flexibility, but in a global business final configuration of the product may take place locally or centrally, depending upon the economies of production, transportation and packaging.

One of the most frequently quoted examples of the application of the postponement concept is that of Benetton, the Italian apparel manufacturer and retailer. Benetton revolutionised the knitwear industry through innovation in the garment manufacturing process, enabling it to hold only one colour of knitwear in stock – plain, undyed grey. This dramatically reduces the amount of inventory held in total, but also improves flexibility as the garments can be dyed to any colour – thus enabling Benetton to meet demand in a myriad of local markets. In a global fashion business with different seasons, trends and local preferences, this degree of flexibility was widely believed to have provided Benetton with a significant marketing edge. However, even Benetton has reappraised its position on 'think global, act local'.

Uniting the Colors of Benetton

Benetton has always been something of a trendsetter in its industry. During the 1980s, it established a worldwide network of retail outlets supplied from its manufacturing base in Northern Italy.

Benetton's manufacturing network was famed for its flexibility. It produced 20 per cent of orders by quick response, with the remaining 80 per cent scheduled to maximise capacity utilisation. However, only those operations (such as design, cutting, dyeing and packing) that brought cost efficiencies through economies of scale, or were deemed essential to product quality, were performed in-house. All other manufacturing (including the labour-intensive finishing stages) was completed by a local network of several hundred suppliers and subcontractors, most of which were small family businesses.

The finished goods were sold through its retail network of around 5500 licensed stores in 120 countries, where its multi-ethnic, multi-coloured 'United Colors of Benetton' advertising campaigns trumpeted its global stance. The product range had originally comprised knitwear and other casual clothing for young adults. Later it went on to broaden its offer with the introduction of several complementary niche brands aimed at babies, children and expectant mothers.

For many years Benetton had balanced the local vs global trade-offs by producing something approximating to a core range, with around 20 per cent of the items customised to meet local requirements – for example, different colour ways for the Middle East and smaller sizes for the Far East. The product mix was also determined by the local retail agents, who selected the designs they felt were most likely to appeal to their own clientele. The result was a global brand with many regional personalities. The strategy worked well, but by the end of the 1990s Benetton was reappraising its position in terms of both marketing and operations.

Benetton believed that globalisation had brought sufficient homogenisation of consumers' lifestyles and market preferences to warrant a new strategy based on a more uniform marketing position, reduced variety and greater economies of scale. The brand portfolio was rationalised to leave only the core 'United Colors of Benetton' and 'Sisley' brands, with collections arranged along the lines of age and sex. The company addressed the disparity in regional brand positioning through the introduction of a more 'globally appealing' product range, with localised content cut to between 5 and 10 per cent. The number of items in the basic seasonal ranges was also reduced by as much as 40 per cent. The potentially negative impact of range reduction was offset by more sophisticated approaches to in-store market research. The number of interim 'flash' collections was also increased, to improve customer-perceived variety.

In terms of operations, the company has extended its supply network beyond the confines of its Italian homeland. The search for lower labour costs has led the company to establish new focused production centres in Spain, Portugal, North Africa, India, Korea, Central Europe and the Balkans. In each region Benetton has recreated its original outsourced manufacturing model, with a cluster of small companies, often set up by ex-Benetton employees or its Italian contractors. The new supplier networks are directly controlled by Benetton through wholly-owned subsidiaries or 50–50 joint ventures. These new production poles use existing local skills to specialise in one particular type of product – for example, jackets are made in Eastern Europe, while Spain focuses on T-shirts. Time will tell whether the customers' needs are indeed homogeneous enough, and Benetton's supply chains agile enough, to support the new strategy.

The second major issue identified above for consideration concerns the deployment and location of inventory holdings within a global supply network. Conventional logistics systems have tended to be based around inventories of fully finished products being held in dispersed locations waiting to be sold. Today's logic of integrated supply chain management suggests that, wherever possible, inventory should be held in as few locations as possible, in as generic a form as possible, to be localised or customised when real demand is identified.

Localising generic products at Hewlett-Packard

In an industry that is characterised by punishingly short product life cycles and extreme unpredictability, getting the right products to the right market on time is an absolute imperative. For computer equipment manufacturer Hewlett-Packard, the need to manufacture and deliver its products quickly, reliably, and ever more cost-effectively led to the development of capabilities that put it at the very forefront of global supply chain management.

Product complexity was a hidden enemy for Hewlett-Packard, for, while the company served a global market place with seemingly global products, these products were almost always tailored to meet local specifications. They had to be delivered with power cords and transformers to meet the local voltage, and supplied with keyboards, manuals and operating software in the appropriate local language. This meant that instead of dealing with a single product line, produced and distributed to meet an overall global forecast, Hewlett-Packard was producing differently configured machines to meet estimated demand in each of a number of relatively small markets. However, the smaller the market, the more erratic the order patterns were likely to be, and the more difficult it was to predict demand accurately.

The uncertainty reverberated back through every stage of the supply chain, wrong-footing internal and external suppliers alike, leading to exaggerated safety stocks and increased risk from obsolete stock or expensive reworking. In the early 1990s there were, for example, five physically separate Hewlett-Packard facilities contributing to the manufacture and distribution of what was then its best-selling family of low-cost 'DeskJet' printers, resulting in a pipeline that was nearly six months long.

Supplying the European market, with its tightly packed cluster of nations and linguistic differences, was particularly troublesome, with huge safety stocks needed to meet Hewlett-Packard's goal of 98 per cent service levels. Product managers, while wishing to lessen their exposure to variability in the supply chain, were eager to reduce the amount of inventory in the system, freeing up cash for other uses. An investigation of how current service levels might be maintained at lower cost was therefore commissioned.

Under the then-current system, the printers were 'localised' at the central factory, ready-packaged for sale in the country of destination. Stockpiles of each of the different language variants were then held at regional distribution centres, ready to meet sudden fluctuations in demand. The question that quickly arose was, what would be the value of switching production over to a single form of generic printer, with 'localisation' postponed until the distribution centre stage?

Hewlett-Packard had been honing its inventory network modelling skills for some time, and was therefore able to apply these skills to modelling the DeskJet supply chain. The results indicated that costs of safety stocks could be significantly reduced if a generic printer was introduced. First, safety stocks could be lowered from seven weeks of finished goods to around five weeks of the generic version, as fewer generic printers would be required to maintain service levels. Secondly, the cost of each unit stockpiled would be reduced because the value added was lower at this point. Anticipated savings were in excess of $30 million per year. The costs associated with performing the localisation process at the distribution centres were slightly higher than if performed by the factory, and higher stocks of localisation materials were required with the dispersal of this activity. Nevertheless, these costs were dwarfed by overall savings on inventory. Furthermore, savings amounting to several million dollars per annum were also identified from reduced shipping costs. The generic printers could be packed more densely and therefore transported more cheaply than before.

The logic of switching to a generic printer for the European market was unimpeachable. The US market already had its own factory-produced version of the generic printer, so ostensibly there seemed to be no case for extending the practice to the US market. Surely there could be no benefit in postponing completion for such a large and homogeneous market? Not so. An extension of the DeskJet study evaluated a proposal to factory produce two versions of the printer; an ultra lost-cost US version, and a generic to serve the rest of the world. This proposal was rejected, however, because of the potential strategic time advantage offered by a single generic printer strategy. The critical factor here was the increased unpredictability of even regional forecasts (for the Americas, Asia, and Europe) when set against a forecast for overall global demand. If, contrary to all earlier indications, demand for a new product failed to materialise in, say, the US, while rest of the world sales took off at an unprecedented rate, pipelines would already be filled to meet predicted demand. A generic printer strategy would allow the immediate diversion of stocks to wherever they were required, at minimal cost and with minimal delay and loss of service. Contrast this with the prospect of reworking unneeded stocks before redirection, or waiting until programmed output could meet demand. In a market with narrowing windows of opportunity, the risk of the latter was deemed to be too great. Hewlett-Packard introduced its global generic printer.

In a multi-product environment the distribution of sales by stock-keeping unit (SKU) tends to conform to the Pareto Rule – i.e. 80 per cent of the volume comes from just 20 per cent of the SKUs. This can be of considerable help when global logistics strategies are being devised. For example, the fastest moving lines (the 20 per cent that provide 80 per cent of the total volume) can be held as finished inventory because demand is likely to be more predictable. These lines can also be carried in local markets, having been shipped there in bulk so as to take advantage of production and transportation scale economies. Because they are fast movers stock-turn will be higher, so in effect only a limited investment in inventory is required. These products should not move through intermediate stock locations such as regional distribution centres, but should be delivered direct.

At the other extreme, the slow-moving products may be held regionally or even centrally and, wherever possible, at a generic level, to be finally configured when precise local requirements are known. Where the value/density of these products and/or their 'critical value' to customers is high (e.g. vital spares), then overnight delivery using specialist service providers such as Fedex, DHL or UPS may be appropriate. These specialist providers have broadened and augmented their own service offers to meet the needs of their global customers, as the DHL/Fujitsu example shows.

DHL helps Fujitsu enhance global service

Fujitsu Personal Systems (FPS) is a wholly owned subsidiary of Fujitsu, headquartered in California, USA. This division of Fujitsu produces handheld computers, of the type used by sales people or service engineers. Manufacturing takes place in Japan, but markets are worldwide.

In order to service their European customers better, Fujitsu established a partnership with DHL. Products flow through the DHL Express Logistics Centre (ELC) in Brussels, Belgium, for overnight delivery to FPS's European customers. The ELC carries out incoming quality and functional inspections, kitting and configuration or repair. The ELC has a 400 square metre technical support facility with a 'clean room' environment. The facility is an approved Fujitsu repair centre manned by qualified technicians, who are employed by DHL having been trained by Fujitsu engineers. All work carried out in the centre carries the full Fujitsu warranty.

Kitting and configuration of products in the ELC enables Fujitsu to hold lower inventories for a given service level, as the ELC is able to customise the basic models and ship the same day. DHL undertakes all order processing and inventory management on behalf of FPS in Europe.

Spare computers are kept in the ELC as partly configured inventory. When a salesman's machine breaks down in the field, the ELC is notified. A spare machine is plugged into the customer's global telecommunications network and receives a download of the appropriate database for that salesman from the customer's mainframe computer in the USA. The ELC technician verifies that the machine functions correctly before it is packed and shipped for next-day delivery to the salesman.

Figure 7.1 suggests some guidelines for the location of inventory in a global network, based upon the volume and the predictability of the item. Using the 80/20 principle, the company can centralise the vast majority of the slow-moving, less predictable lines, achieving a considerable reduction in total inventory. Almost certainly the reduction in inventory carrying costs will more than compensate for the higher cost of express delivery.

The third and final issue referred to earlier in this section is the question of where the forecast should be made. In one sense, the closer to the point of final demand the better it is to forecast in order that local conditions can be factored into the equation. However, these local

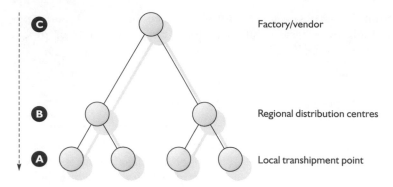

Factory/vendor

Regional distribution centres

Local transhipment point

Key:

Ⓐ Direct shipment of fast-moving, predictable lines. Held locally, probably pre-configured

Ⓑ Inventory of medium velocity, less predictable demand lines held at generic level awaiting final configuration

Ⓒ Slowest moving lines, least predictable. Perhaps one shared global inventory or make to order

Figure 7.1 Inventory location in a global network

forecasts will inevitably be prone to more error than an aggregate forecast made further up the chain.

Hewlett-Packard found that it was better to forecast sales at a generic level (i.e. an aggregate European forecast) and to hold stock prior to localisation in a generic form. The same principle holds true for many other kinds of products. Gillette, for example, the branded manufacturer of grooming and dental products, writing instruments and small electrical appliances, competes worldwide in FMCG categories, where promotional activity means that demand is notoriously volatile. Some years ago Gillette opted to centralise European purchasing, inventory holding and forecasting, leaving only the promotionally-dependent packaging requirements to be driven by national item level forecasts. The same generic inventory can then be used to satisfy local demand with the addition of local language wrap-over packaging, promotional packs or whatever.

Global logistics information systems

It will be apparent that to implement these ideas of flexible response through postponement and localisation requires the ability to 'see' from one end of the logistics pipeline to the other. Global visibility enables logistics management to manage the flow of product better and to optimise production and transportation capacity whilst keeping inventory to a minimum.

Companies like Benetton are able to read demand on a daily basis from each of their worldwide markets, and can plan production and delivery accordingly. They are aided in this by the advent of global logistics information systems, which enable sales to be monitored in real time, shipments to be tracked, purchase orders to be issued and production schedules to be monitored, with the result that the 'pipeline' can be much better managed.

A significant benefit of achieving end-to-end supply chain visibility in a global context is the opportunities for improvement that become apparent once bottlenecks are highlighted and the inventory buffers – created as a result of lack of information – are revealed. For example, Toys 'R' Us, the USA-based toy retailer, monitors its product flow from offshore suppliers (mainly Far Eastern) into its worldwide retail outlets, literally from door to door. A third party global logistics service provider not only manages the transportation but also, through its tracking and tracing system, is able to keep Toys 'R' Us informed of the precise location of every container and its contents. Information from the moment the product leaves the Asian factories is fed to the toy company, so that two weeks before the cargo arrives in North America it can inform the retail stores of what is coming, potential delays and missing product, enabling stores to manage their inventories better and to re-order as necessary. Inventory savings are estimated in millions of dollars as a result.

More recently we have seen the formation of B2B exchanges, established to utilise the power of the Internet to facilitate transactions and the flow of information between these global players. Early examples were CPG markets.com, serving the packaged consumer goods manufacturers and their suppliers; Transora, which is a B2B market place for the global food and packaged goods industry; and Worldwide Retail Exchange, a grouping of major retailers.

Whilst it is difficult to predict the future development of international exchanges, it is certain that the landscape of competition in FMCG markets in the years ahead will be vastly different from the one we see today. What is not in question is that the retailers who are trading in these intensely competitive environments are devoting more resources to challenging costs as supply chains become the key battleground. This is set to sharpen distinctions between price-driven and value-added trading relationships.

In the food retailing sector the trend is towards aggregated purchasing power on a national and regional basis, although few have yet made the transition to truly global purchasing. Those leading international suppliers who have not yet established global account teams to liaise with central buying teams are expected to do so.

Questions of sustainability

The trend towards global sourcing in almost everything, from car components to fresh produce, shows no signs of abating. This, and the prevailing tendency towards outsourcing to suppliers operating in low-wage manufacturing centres, has raised questions about the environmental and social implications of globalisation. It should also raise fundamental questions about the limitations and perhaps the long-term viability of lean, just-in-time manufacturing and supply chain strategies.

The environmental impact of lengthening supply chains is a matter of concern amongst a growing number of European consumers, lobby groups and government agencies. 'Transport 2000', an environmental organisation whose agenda involves the development of more sustainable transport policies, has led the debate in the UK. Their *Wise Moves* initiative rallied support from a wide spectrum of non-governmental agencies, academics and leading representatives of the retail community in their efforts to identify whether local sourcing of goods would lead to an overall increase or decrease in greenhouse gas emissions along the whole food supply chain. There are indications that local sourcing could indeed reduce the environmental damage. Leading representatives of the business community, although willing in principle to support local sourcing, make it clear that they would be unable to do so unless a clear business case could be made for such a move. Consumer attitudes, national/international policy developments, and the questions relating to the vulnerability of global supply networks are all part of this equation.

The vulnerability of global supply chains

Over recent years the drive towards leaner, more consolidated, more efficient supply chain networks has succeeded in driving excess inventory out of many supply systems. The approach has been particularly successful in industries where demand is relatively stable, and where physical and information infrastructures are efficient and above all reliable. However, the removal of 'buffer' stocks has been so complete that in some instances there is nothing left in the system to deal with any interruptions in supply. The events of the year 2001 showed the world that these disruptions could arise anywhere, at any time, from any number of sources – including accidents, natural disasters or acts of armed aggression. They could also arise from more mundane occurrences, such as new product introductions in seemingly unrelated industries.

The outbreak of foot and mouth disease in 2001 was widely recognised as having seriously affected the UK's livestock and tourism industries. However, a study undertaken by the Cranfield Centre for Logistics and Transportation on behalf of the DTLR, DTI and Home Office (*Supply Chain Vulnerability*, January 2002) found that companies in industries as diverse as brewing, car manufacturing and healthcare had all been affected by this and other livestock diseases.

The research revealed that as a result of BSE, the brain disease first found in UK cattle in the 1990s, a global healthcare company had been forced to reconfigure its global supply chains totally, effectively dividing its global market place into two following the banning of imports of UK-sourced blood products into the USA.

During the foot and mouth epidemic, a Dutch-based brewer had found its production threatened by its inability to either store or dispose of spent grain – a by-product of the brewing process. The grain would normally have been taken for animal feed. Meanwhile, in continental Europe a luxury car manufacturer was struggling to source the high quality leather it required for seats.

The second massively disruptive event of the year 2001 was the closure of North American airspace immediately after the terrorist attacks on New York and Washington on 11 September. This and the closure of the country's borders caused immediate disruptions to many industries in North America and beyond. North American car plants were halted as borders were closed, cutting off supplies of vital components, whilst on the other side of the Atlantic leading UK supermarkets scrambled to find alternative supplies of fresh produce from unaffected parts of the world.

Less dramatic, but no less disruptive to the organisations concerned, were sudden shortages of key ingredients or components caused by new product launches in seemingly unrelated industries. A British-based aerospace manufacturer experienced such a problem when it was suddenly left without supplies of titanium for its aircraft, as a result of the massively successful new product launch by the world's leading manufacturer of golf clubs. An internationally known manufacturer of office equipment had a similar experience, when production of its printers was halted by the launch of the Sony PlayStation. The two products shared a common computer chip, but Sony was the larger of the single supplier's customers.

The social aspects of global sourcing go hand in hand with the environmental and wider 'ethical' concerns. Consumer groups throughout Europe now actively lobby for, amongst other things, 'fair trade' policies and forward-looking solutions to help impoverished children employed in the higher reaches of globally outsourced supply networks.

Closer to home for many consumers are the social consequences of the job losses that have accompanied the internationalisation of markets, outsourcing, and the steady progress towards global procurement.

Rover, the UK's last indigenous carmaker, was a textbook favourite, an example of how a failing nationalised manufacturer could make the transition to attractive takeover target. Rover appeared to have overcome the threats of global competition by adopting the lean production, supplier development, and quality improvement practices of its Japanese rivals. The company had, of course, inherited some of the most internationally desirable heritage motoring brands, as well as the world-renowned Land Rover company.

Few doubted that, by remodelling itself along the lines of the 'extended enterprise', Rover had transformed itself from a model of inefficiency and worst practice industrial relations to become a viable concern. However, with the benefit of hindsight this seems to have offered little more than a temporary reprieve. Following its acquisition by Germany's BMW, the enterprise began to unravel as Rover became increasingly unviable and worldwide the industry continued to consolidate and shifted to global sourcing. In March 2000, the remains of Rover were sold for £10 to a consortium led by its former chief executive. The sale saved Rover from immediate annihilation, and provided a temporary reprieve for an estimated 54 000 jobs in the English West Midlands.

The automotive industry has in many ways been a bell-wether of globalisation. In terms of supply chain structures, it seems that where the car industry leads, other mature industries are fated to follow.

In the USA and the UK, the impact of globalisation on the textile and apparel industries has also been hotly debated. The case of Milliken and the birth of integrated 'quick response' logistics was discussed in Chapter 5. The solution there was a more integrated, more tightly coupled supply chain. In the UK, the *cause célèbre* was the decision by Marks & Spencer (M&S) not to seek closer relationships with its leading suppliers – it already had them – but to forsake them to seek new lower-cost suppliers elsewhere.

M&S had in fact been operating its own version of an 'extended enterprise' long before the first Japanese car ever landed on British soil. Its partnership approach to supplier management had made it another textbook favourite, and its name a byword for quality, service and value for money. However, in 1998 things suddenly went badly wrong for Europe's most profitable retailer. Out-of-touch management, complacency in marketing and, above all, an ossified supply chain were subsequently identified as root causes of M&S's problems.

The retailer – and more so its dedicated apparel suppliers – lost out to new overseas competitors, whose flexible and extensive supply networks were better able to cope with the challenges of internationalisation. Hong Kong-based company Li & Fung (L&F) orchestrates one of the largest and most successful of these networks, supplying the retail chains of Europe and North America with private label products. L&F does not produce any of the goods it supplies; it is a trader and – in the parlance of networks – a network broker. The company's knowledge of the apparel industry supply chain and its extensive contacts have allowed it to build a network spanning 39 countries and comprising over 6000 highly specialised production firms. Collectively, these firms constitute a vast pool of expertise and a huge and infinitely flexible manufacturing resource.

L&F can draw upon this resource base as required, configuring networks of highly skilled specialists to meet precise requirements of each job. The network broker co-ordinates the manufacturing and delivery process from end-to-end – not by tightly micro-managing every detail of production, but by selecting trusted specialists to perform each step, from sourcing raw materials through design, manufacture, shipping and all the way to final delivery. It manages the interfaces between these organisations, specifying the exact requirements and timescale for each step, but leaving the suppliers to manage the detail of how that is achieved. In this way the supplier is encouraged to manage its own efficiency and to innovate within its own sphere. L&F retains the co-operation of its suppliers by taking between 30 and 70 per cent of their production capacity. Quality is monitored at various milestones along the way.

If problems arise with any particular aspect of the process, the work can quickly be switched to another of L&F's many providers. The ability to reconfigure the network at short notice together with the fact that it is geographically dispersed is among its great strengths. For example, after the terrorist attacks of 11 September 2001, hundreds of millions of dollars worth of manufacturing was switched at very short notice from areas that were considered to be 'high risk' to more stable manufacturing locations.

L&F has expanded the scope of its network from apparel into other high-volume time-sensitive consumer goods, including fashion accessories, shoes, toys, sports equipment and home furnishings, but always retains responsibility for the final product and customer interface.

Dismantling Marks & Spencer's extended enterprise

In June 1997 M&S's retail empire stretched to 651 locations across 31 countries, although its power base was its home market in the UK. It was the UK's leading retailer of lingerie, men's suits and classic-styled ladies outerwear, shoes and jeans.

The company readily acknowledged that its achievements owed much to long-standing partnerships with its leading suppliers. M&S designed most of its clothes in-house, before putting the designs forward to favoured manufacturers along with notoriously strict specifications regarding the finished product.

The manufacturers provided dedicated facilities for M&S, who required suppliers to refrain from bidding for work from other clients. The close partnership arrangements also alleviated the need for M&S to allocate resources of its own to technological research and development activities. Instead, the retailer relied on its trusted suppliers to put forward their most recent innovations – often allowing M&S exclusive access to technological breakthroughs. Decades of experience had taught the suppliers that their reward for servicing such a demanding client was a culture of continuous improvement within their businesses, and the loyalty of M&S through good times and bad.

The physical distribution of merchandise had been outsourced for decades to specialist suppliers. The UK was the hub of all distribution activities, but the retailer was keen to improve the efficiency of these operations. It was also aware that it could not continue to service its international retail network solely from the UK. The UK-centric sourcing and supply strategy was inhibiting the development of the business in Asia and the Pacific.

M&S still officially encouraged its suppliers to source in the UK, enabling it to maintain its 'buy British' marketing stance. However, the suppliers were struggling to remain price-competitive. Some had opted to supply at least a proportion of M&S's orders from overseas facilities. They would buy in virtually finished goods produced in low-cost manufacturing centres such as China, then ship them to the UK for finishing. Some of the consignment would then be returned to the region of origin for sale. The round trip lengthened the delay before goods appeared in the shops, and in some instances added as much as £14 to an item that cost only £4 to make. The additional cost incurred, together with the strengthening pound, was forcing M&S to position itself much further upmarket overseas than its middle-market positioning in the UK.

M&S had always been a mainstream mass-market retailer, but was mindful of consultants' reports predicting the long-term decline of the middle market. The situation worsened dramatically in the summer of 1998, when M&S's buyers had made a catastrophic misjudgement about the forthcoming year's fashion trends. They had bet on black and grey being the season's colours, but consumers disagreed. M&S's famously loyal customers flocked instead to the stores of international niche retailers such as the US-based Gap and Spain's rapidly expanding high fashion chain Zara.

M&S had always operated on the basis of two clothing collections per year, using massive-scale forward planning to place orders with a few favoured suppliers approximately nine months ahead of the season. In contrast, rivals such as the Gap, Zara or the Swedish chain H&M's fashion-savvy buyers worked on quick turn-round systems.

To win back the lost customers, M&S decided to lower prices of its core product range for the forthcoming season (autumn/winter 1999) by up to 20 per cent. It looked to its suppliers for the necessary cost reductions. The retailer began notifying them that they would also be required to relocate a substantial proportion of their M&S production capacity overseas. The economics of manufacturing many product categories in the UK were becoming untenable when costs were compared with those in Asia. M&S went on to announce its intention to reduce the number of suppliers in an attempt to give fewer suppliers longer (and cheaper) production runs.

Amongst those to be dropped at short notice was William Baird, the smallest of M&S's 'big four' suppliers, behind Courtaulds Textiles, Dewhirst, and Coats Viyella. Between them the four companies supplied more than 60 per cent of M&S's clothing stock. Baird was the least exposed of the big four, but had publicly criticised M&S clothes buying systems, alleging that they were riddled with inefficiencies. There were also claims that clothing orders that could have been turned around in four weeks were taking eight months to reach M&S showrooms.

Baird's business later plunged £93.5 million into the red, having taken an exceptional charge of £103 million to cover the closure of its M&S clothing division. Two years earlier Baird had had 21 factories in the UK, 20 of them dedicated to supplying M&S. Five factories had already been closed, as production was shifted to three facilities in Sri Lanka. Of the remaining 16, some – including a newly-opened £4.2 million bra factory in Somerset – were taken over by rival suppliers, although most were to close with a loss of 4500 jobs.

Baird went on to sue M&S for breach of contract, even though, like most of M&S's longest-standing suppliers, Baird had no formal contract with its key customer. The High Court ruled against Baird's claim that the 30-year trading relationship between the two companies constituted an implied long-term contract.

It was planned that the bulk of Baird's work would be transferred to the retailer's other three core suppliers. However, Courtaulds Textiles was having problems of its own. It was the biggest supplier of women's underwear and hosiery to M&S, and had been for more than 50 years. In February 2000 it too had become a bid target after turning in poor end-of-year results. Sales of its hosiery and underwear to M&S were down 17 per cent on the previous year, and profits were down 60 per cent. Top management readily admitted that it had lost control of its key M&S business for several months in 1999 as the company struggled to deal with the move to overseas sourcing.

In planning the overseas moves few had stopped to consider the possible impact of political upheavals and local wars on the relocation plans. Nor had they anticipated a shortage of available freight capacity, or of textile import quotas. The issue of quotas became a major problem when managers discovered that Sri Lanka (M&S's favoured location) had used up its entire annual textile quota by June.

Then there were the difficulties arising from attempts to switch suppliers over to FOB (free-on-board) terms of supply. M&S had hitherto bought from its suppliers on a DDP (duty delivery paid) basis, with an agreed price per item. Some manufacturers were also reluctant to abandon existing transport agreements and switch to M&S preferred transport suppliers.

Supplier relationships were becoming more strained than ever. However, further price cuts were required. Analysts calculated that these could cost the larger suppliers up to £1 million each. M&S argued that it simply had no choice but to seek financial support from its suppliers in its efforts to give customers better value. For Coats Viyella, this was a step too far. Having already sustained heavy losses on its M&S clothing business, it announced that it was to end its 70-year relationship with M&S. Around 80 per cent of Coats' business was with M&S, but after consideration the supplier decided that it would not relocate existing facilities overseas to meet M&S's requests. The retailer would have to switch the work to another supplier.

In September 2000, M&S announced that, although changes in buying practices had improved margins in some parts of its clothing business, sales of women's wear and lingerie were still depressed. The problem was particularly acute within the lingerie business where, despite favourable reactions to the new ranges, sales had fallen due to poor availability.

Control of the customer interface – preferably the final customer interface – is increasingly being recognised as a key determinant of success for the orchestrators of global networks.

The shift in power from large FMCG branded manufacturers to retailers is well documented, and has been discussed at intervals throughout this book. In those sectors where the balance of power has not yet shifted irrevocably downstream, powerful manufacturers are turning once more to vertical integration to gain control of the end-customer interface.

This trend has also been apparent in a number of industries, from apparel to pharmaceuticals. Car manufacturers have over recent years struggled to wrest control of the high value-adding after-sales service opportunities from long-established franchise dealerships. The astute, like Benetton or the groundbreaking Millennium Pharmaceuticals, also recognise that their long-term competitiveness is ultimately dependent on meeting the needs, wants and desires of the final consumer.

Benetton and Millennium both have considerable expertise in network management and, mindful of global trends, have elected to take an active role in reshaping the way value is created within their industries. Benetton, having revolutionised the knitwear production process, has turned to vertical integration to ensure responsiveness elsewhere in its supply chain. It has purchased and consolidated textile producers upstream of its garment manufacturing networks, thus controlling supply and quality of its inbound raw materials. This has allowed the company to extend its control of logistics processes higher up the supply chain, and thus to influence quality at an earlier point. It has also reduced overall production lead times.

Benetton has also taken direct control of its retail outlets, abandoning a long-standing strategy that entrusted retailing to independent franchisees. The aggressive market-penetration strategies of new entrants, with much larger store formats, were marginalising Benetton. Larger outlets allowed entire (albeit reduced) collections to be displayed, providing the company with a much more accurate indication of demand and emerging market trends.

Millennium Pharmaceuticals, a business start-up founded in 1994, is leading the way towards personalised medicine, creating drugs against end-consumers' own genetic profiles. Millennium, like Benetton, applied technological innovation to established processes – in this instance it automated the process of research into basic genes and proteins – at the earliest stage in the development of new drugs to tackle the causes rather than the symptoms of genetically related diseases. This in turn has led to a dramatic reduction in cycle times for the identification and testing of 'leads' for embryonic new drugs. The breakthrough has altered the economics of drug development.

Rather than limiting itself to harvesting the value from its unique core competence in only the very highest reaches of the pharmaceutical supply chain, Millennium has skilfully managed an array of alliances with other established industry players to follow a strategy of downstream vertical integration. This has allowed it to capitalise on the added value from its technological breakthrough as its impact migrates along the value chain. Millennium's founders were aware that to deliver its ultimate strategic goal – personalised medicine – it must understand the impact of its fledgling drugs on real patients. To do that, it must have direct access to their gene profiles.

Millennium, like Benetton, is an organisation that understands the need to match its structure to its strategy, which in turn is based on delivering real value to its customers. These organisations, and others like them, will no doubt continue to evolve in pursuit of their goals. Their supply and distribution networks, whether tightly or loosely coupled (or indeed a mixture of both), must be capable of creating and delivering products and services in an efficient and effective way. To do so they must strive to manage demand as well as supply. In a global market place they must be innovative and agile enough to shape as well as respond to changes in demand, technology, regulation or tariff, and be resilient enough to deal with all manner of external disruptions.

Serving the global customer: key issues

- The growth of the global corporation
  - The rise of the global customer and the global brand
  - Internationalisation of manufacturing and retailing
  - Consolidation, rationalisation and focused manufacturing

- Developing a global logistics strategy
  - Should we manage centrally or locally?
  - The search for global synergy
  - The basic question: to standardise or customise?

- Meeting local needs whilst seeking global economies
  - The opportunities for localisation through 'postponement'
  - Where should inventory be carried?
  - Where should the forecast be made?

- Globalisation and the network organisation
  - Global logistics information systems
  - Outsourced supply networks: environmental and social issues
  - The vulnerability of longer, consolidated supply chains
  - Tightly coupled and loosely coupled networks

Index

Marketing titles from Butterworth-Heinemann

Student List

Creating Powerful Brands (second edition), Leslie de Chernatony and Malcolm McDonald

Direct Marketing in Practice, Brian Thomas and Matthew Housden

eMarketing eXcellence, PR Smith and Dave Chaffey

Fashion Marketing, Margaret Bruce and Tony Hines

Innovation in Marketing, Peter Doyle and Susan Bridgewater

Integrated Marketing Communications, Tony Yeshin

Internal Marketing, Pervaiz Ahmed and Mohammed Rafiq

International Marketing (third edition), Stanley J. Paliwoda and Michael J. Thomas

Key Customers, Malcolm McDonald, Beth Rogers and Diana Woodburn

Marketing Briefs, Sally Dibb and Lyndon Simkin

Marketing in Travel and Tourism (third edition), Victor T. C. Middleton with Jackie R. Clarke

Marketing Logistics (second edition), Martin Christopher and Helen Peck

Marketing Plans (fifth edition), Malcolm McDonald

Marketing Research for Managers (third edition), Sunny Crouch and Matthew Housden

Marketing: the One Semester Introduction, Geoff Lancaster and Paul Reynolds

Market-Led Strategic Change (third edition), Nigel Piercy

Relationship Marketing (second edition), Martin Christopher, Adrian Payne and David Ballantyne

Relationship Marketing for Competitive Advantage, Adrian Payne, Martin Christopher, Moira Clark and Helen Peck

Relationship Marketing: Strategy & Implementation, Helen Peck, Adrian Payne, Martin Christopher and Moira Clark

Strategic Marketing Management (second edition), Richard M. S. Wilson and Colin Gilligan

Strategic Marketing: Planning and Control (second edition), Graeme Drummond and John Ensor

Successful Marketing Communications, Cathy Ace

Tales from the Market Place, Nigel Piercy

The CIM Handbook of Export Marketing, Chris Noonan

The Fundamentals of Advertising (second edition), John Wilmshurst and Adrian Mackay

The Fundamentals and Practice of Marketing (fourth edition), John Wilmshurst and Adrian Mackay

The Marketing Book (fifth edition), Michael J. Baker (ed.)
The New Marketing, Malcolm McDonald and Hugh Wilson
Total Relationship Marketing (second edition), Evert Gummesson

Forthcoming
Marketing Strategy (third edition), Paul Fifield
Political Marketing, Phil Harris and Dominic Wring

Professional List
Cause Related Marketing, Sue Adkins
Creating Value, Shiv S. Mathur and Alfred Kenyon
Cybermarketing (second edition), Pauline Bickerton and Matthew Bickerton
Cyberstrategy, Pauline Bickerton, Matthew Bickerton and Kate
    Simpson-Holley
Direct Marketing in Practice, Brian Thomas and Matthew Housden
e-Business, J. A. Matthewson
Effective Promotional Practice for eBusiness, Cathy Ace
Essential Law for Marketers, Ardi Kolah
Excellence in Advertising (second edition), Leslie Butterfield
Fashion Marketing, Margaret Bruce and Tony Hines
Financial Services and the Multimedia Revolution, Paul Lucas, Rachel
    Kinniburgh and Donna Terp
From Brand Vision to Brand Evaluation, Leslie de Chernatony
Go to Market Strategy, Lawrence Friedman
Internal Marketing, Pervaiz Ahmed and Mohammed Rafiq
Marketing Logistics (second edition), Martin Christopher and Helen Peck
Marketing Made Simple, Geoff Lancaster and Paul Reynolds
Marketing Professional Services, Michael Roe
Marketing Research for Managers (third edition), Sunny Crouch and Matthew
    Housden
Marketing Strategy (second edition), Paul Fifield
Market-Led Strategic Change (third edition), Nigel Piercy
The Channel Advantage, Lawrence Friedman and Tim Furey
The CIM Handbook of Export Marketing, Chris Noonan
The Committed Enterprise, Hugh Davidson
The Fundamentals of Corporate Communications, Richard Dolphin
The Marketing Plan in Colour, Malcolm McDonald and Peter Morris
The New Marketing, Malcolm McDonald and Hugh Wilson

Forthcoming
Marketing Strategy (third edition), Paul Fifield
Political Marketing, Phil Harris and Dominic Wring

For more information on all these titles, as well as the ability to buy
online, please visit **www.bh.com/marketing**